Magna Carta: A Very Short Introduction

VERY SHORT INTRODUCTIONS are for anyone wanting a stimulating and accessible way in to a new subject. They are written by experts and have been translated into more than 40 different languages. The series began in 1995 and now covers a wide variety of topics in every discipline. The VSI library contains nearly 400 volumes—a Very Short Introduction to everything from Indian philosophy to psychology and American history—and continues to grow in every subject area.

Very Short Introductions available now:

Nicholas Vincent

MAGNA CARTA

A Very Short Introduction

OXFORD
UNIVERSITY PRESS

OXFORD
UNIVERSITY PRESS

Great Clarendon Street, Oxford OX2 6DP,
United Kingdom

Oxford University Press is a department of the University of Oxford.
It furthers the University's objective of excellence in research, scholarship,
and education by publishing worldwide. Oxford is a registered trade mark of
Oxford University Press in the UK and in certain other countries

© Nicholas Vincent 2012

The moral rights of the author have been asserted

First Edition Published in 2012

Impression: 4

British Library Cataloguing in Publication Data
Data available

Library of Congress Cataloging in Publication Data
Data available

ISBN 978-0-19-958287-7

Printed in Great Britain by
Ashford Colour Press Ltd, Gosport, Hampshire

For Paul Redfern
legis aquilae executorique

Contents

List of illustrations

Acknowledgements

The present study was begun at Les Jardies and completed in Rouen in May 2011, one of several unexpected consequences of an invitation to play a part in the sale of the Magna Carta auctioned in New York in 2007. For that invitation, I am indebted to Christopher de Hamel, James Stourton, Tim Bolton, and above all to David Redden. What I know of Magna Carta I owe to the teaching of John Maddicott. I have also drawn heavily upon the expertise of Paul Brand, David Carpenter, and Sir James Holt. Hugh Doherty acted as an enthusiastic runner. Sophie Poirey invited me to consider the charter's Norman connections, again with unexpected consequences. My colleagues in Norwich have, as always, offered an inexhaustible supply of wisdom and convivial dissent.

Norwich, December 2011

A very short introduction

English history is more often recited as a procession of kings and queens than of documents or ideas. As is well known, Britain has no written constitution. Yet just as historians of America or France have fetishized pieces of paper or parchment – declarations of the Rights of Men or of republican Independence – for the history of England there are at least three or four documentary relics that all students might be expected to name. The 1086 Domesday Book would be one, the Great Reform Act of 1832 another. A third might be the 1689 Bill of Rights. At their head, looming over all others, would stand the object that forms the subject of this present enquiry: Magna Carta, literally 'the Great Charter', first issued by King John of England in 1215.

In its earliest incarnation, as an undertaking by the king to observe certain liberties granted to God, the Church, and the free men of England, Magna Carta takes the form of a single sheet of parchment – dried and smoothed sheepskin – on which, in ink manufactured from water, dust, and powdered oak-apple, are written some 4,000 words of medieval Latin. The outcome is an object by no means beautiful to behold. Today, only four examples of the original 1215 Magna Carta charter survive. Flattened out, each occupies roughly the same surface area as a standard modern television screen. At the bottom hung – and in the case of one of the surviving examples still hangs – an impression of the king's seal, in green or brown beeswax. The unique surviving example of a sealed 1215 Magna Carta, now in the British Library in London, was so badly damaged by fire in the 1730s that its seal has been reduced to a shapeless lump, today looking like nothing so much as a piece of chewed-up toffee. It is on the basis of these unlovely objects that a vast edifice of political and constitutional rhetoric has been built.

The merest glance at the newspapers or at modern political debate would reveal the semi-mythical status that Magna Carta still commands in England and the English-speaking world. 'The foundation of the freedom of the individual against the arbitrary authority of the despot' (Lord Denning); 'The great cornerstone in England's temple of liberty' (Jerome K. Jerome, whose *Three Men in a Boat*, it may be remembered, were notoriously unable to pitch a tent on the site of Runnymede): these and many more such plaudits have been loaded onto a document more often appealed to than actually read. A fortnight after D-Day, in June 1944, King George VI was travelling back to Windsor Castle, inveighing against the latest infringement of royal prerogative by the wartime government of Winston Churchill. 'Suddenly', his secretary reports, 'he threw his arm out of the window and exclaimed "And that's where it all started!"'. The royal car was just passing Runnymede.

Magna Carta is generally (though, as we shall see, wrongly) supposed to be the first attempt to codify English law. As such, it is still cited in English and American law courts. Even within the past decade, attempts have been made to employ one or other of its clauses to argue points of principle, from fundamental matters of public interest such as the detention of those suspected of terrorism, or the right to silence for the accused in criminal trials, down to private grievances over fishing rights on the rivers Severn or Shannon. As recently as January 2012, a group of New Hampshire Republicans presented a bill intended to ensure that any new state legislation affecting individual rights or liberties incorporate a quotation from Magna Carta.

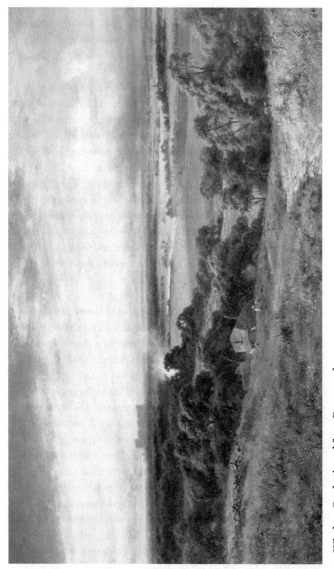

1. Windsor Castle viewed from Runnymede

In fact, surprisingly little of the original Magna Carta remains on today's statute book. As issued in 1215, Magna Carta was first and foremost a peace treaty between king and barons, not an enunciation of abstract 'laws'. Although it survived the immediate circumstances of its issue, nearly one-third of its words were either dropped or substantially rewritten within the first ten years of its existence. As a result, the charter as received by later lawyers and historians is a hybrid brought about through a series of reissues early in the reign of King John's son, Henry III. By the 1980s, as a result of law reform, all but four of Magna Carta's original sixty clauses had been declared obsolete, erased from the statute book. What remain are the clauses granting freedom to the Church (clause 1), guaranteeing the customs and liberties of the city of London (clause 13), and a more general prohibition (clauses 39–40) disclaiming the king's power to order arbitrary arrest, forbidding the sale of justice, and guaranteeing judgment by a person's equals (or 'peers') – in other words, what we might think of today as the right to trial by jury.

Despite the long after-life of these clauses, the charter as a whole was already treated as an archaic relic as long ago as 1300, when it was for the last time granted a full reissue by a king of England, King John's grandson Edward I. By then, it had already become more a totemic monument to past struggles than something tailored to current political circumstance. Yet as the reissues of the 13th century demonstrate, Magna Carta remained of immense importance to the political community. By 1218, it had already acquired its sobriquet as the 'great' ('Magna') charter. By the 1230s, its defence had become the principal rallying point for the king's subjects against the arbitrary authority of the crown. In the 1620s, it was revived as a political manifesto, cited by Parliamentarians as a check upon the Stuart kings and their claims to 'absolute' power. In the 18th century, it was proudly exhibited as one of the greater treasures of the newly established British Museum (subsequently the British Library). In 2007, when for the very first time an 'original' Magna Carta, albeit one from the late reissue of 1297, came up for public auction, not only did it attract worldwide media attention and a remarkable price ($21.3 million, the highest ever paid for a single sheet of parchment), but the crowds that queued to see it, in New York where it was put on sale, and elsewhere, in Oxford or Lincoln or Salisbury or London or Canberra, wherever other 'original' Magna Cartas are publicly displayed, bore witness to a continuing fascination with this most remarkable of documentary relics. Even today, to enter the hushed gallery where the British Library's original Magna Cartas are exhibited is to experience a sense of semi-religious awe.

It is to explain the true meaning of this document, to elucidate the circumstances in which it was issued, and to trace something of the subsequent memorialization of Magna Carta, that this book has been written. Most of what follows is a restatement of truths established by other historians, as a result of nearly six centuries of scholarly investigation. From time to time, however, it is possible to improve upon our understanding, to bring new connections to light, and even in one instance (the so-called 'committee' of 25 barons) to reveal a truth that has lain hidden since the 13th century. Any appreciation of Magna Carta must begin with an understanding of the circumstances of the reign of King John, and to understand the reign of King John we in turn need to appreciate the historical context. To do this, we shall find ourselves tunnelling backwards from 1215 towards the origins of English law in Anglo-Saxon, Roman, and ultimately in even more ancient traditions.

Chapter 1
In Good King Edward's golden days

According to A. A. Milne, the author of *Winnie the Pooh*, King John was not a good man: 'he had his little ways'. King John's 'little ways' have earned him a prominent place in the pantheon of infamy. It was to curb them that Magna Carta was first devised. From television explorations of 'The Most Evil Men in History', to Ridley Scott's *Robin Hood*, King John has generally been portrayed as the most gruesome of pantomime villains. His reputation for duplicity and worse is at least seven centuries old. Writing in the 1230s, the English chronicler Matthew Paris declared that 'Black as is Hell, John's presence there makes it blacker still'. These sentiments were enthusiastically echoed by 19th-century historians who became the first properly to explore the chronicles and documentary evidence for John's reign. According to William Stubbs, doyen of this Victorian school of history, King John, who 'defied God by word and deed all his life', was polluted by every sin that could disgrace a man. Attempts since the 1960s to rehabilitate King John, to suggest, for example, that he was a competent military commander and a more than competent administrator, have not fared well. Instead, the modern consensus is best summed up in John Gillingham's memorable phrase, 'King John was a shit!'. There have been at least twenty-three popes named John (twenty-five if one counts the two John Pauls), two kings of France, six of Portugal, and no fewer than eight emperors of Byzantium. There has been only one

King John of England. When it was rumoured, in the 1370s, that John of Gaunt, duke of Lancaster, was about to claim the throne of England, usurping the rights of his nephew, Richard II, it was Gaunt's inauspicious name that inspired the outcry 'No more King John!'. It was the crimes of the original King John that led directly to Magna Carta, but to understand those crimes – they included, so the story goes, murder, adultery, apostasy, treachery, and, worst of all, incompetence – we need to return to the 12th century and to the family, the Plantagenets, from which John sprang. Magna Carta was not merely a response to the crimes of one particular king. It was directed against the excesses of an entire dynasty.

King John was the youngest of the six legitimate sons of King Henry II of England. He and his brothers sprang from a family that was French in language and culture. Their father, King Henry II, was the first member of the Plantagenet dynasty (named, perhaps, from the family's symbol, the broom plant or 'plante de gênet') to have ruled over England, yet Henry was born not the son of a king but merely as the eldest of the three sons of Geoffrey count of Anjou, ruler of Angers and the cities of the Loire valley placed under 'Angevin' (from Angers/Anjou) authority. The rule of Henry II and his sons is therefore known collectively as 'Plantagenet' or 'Angevin' kingship, and in the minds of historians 'Angevin kingship' is necessarily associated with arbitrary or brute royal power, in the ultimate extreme with what contemporaries would characterize as Plantagenet 'tyranny'.

Nineteenth-century historians were inclined to regard the Plantagenets as alien 'Frenchmen' imposed upon a freedom-loving English population. But this is drastically to underestimate the complexity of medieval English society. In reality, by the 1120s, let alone by the 1190s, the 'English' barons were themselves a mongrel breed of French, Norman, and Anglo-Saxon descent. Bi- or trilingual (in French, Latin, and English), they were lords of a cross-Channel polity, in which the wealth of England supported adventures as far south as the Loire or the Pyrenees. England had undergone a traumatic Norman Conquest after 1066, but it would be wrong to suppose that this marked a complete break in English history or that Norman and English traditions of law and government were thereafter strictly segregated. On the contrary, the customary laws of the Anglo-Saxons were to a large extent preserved, including most famously the idea of the jury of twelve men, responsible in English law from at least the 1160s until 1879 not just as a 'trial jury' for determining guilt or innocence but as a 'jury of presentment' for 'presenting' suspected criminals for trial (in some ways equivalent to the modern American 'Grand Jury', for the investigation, not merely the trial of wrongdoing). English techniques of government were readily adopted by the new Norman conquerors and were exported to Normandy. For example, the kings of England before 1066 had routinely communicated their instructions to the localities via 'writs' (brief written mandates). This was a technique unknown to the Norman dukes, but by the 1120s had become ubiquitous in Normandy as in England.

What was peculiar about the Plantagenet as opposed to the Norman kings was not their Frenchness but the particular part of France from which they derived. The county of Anjou had long been regarded as a rival to the duchy of Normandy from which the majority of the new lords of the Anglo-Norman empire sprang. Even so, it would be risky to suppose too clear an apartheid between accents or provincial allegiances. Nor were all Frenchmen necessarily seen as the pledged enemies of English freedoms. 'Liberty' may to some extent already have been regarded as an especially English birth-right. It was for their victories against the 'tyrants' of the late-Roman world that the Anglo-Saxon peoples had been commemorated, not least by the Venerable Bede, the most influential of early medieval chroniclers. Monks and churchmen of the 8th century, reacting against the stern authority of King Offa, began to embellish their title deeds with claims to 'liberty' conceived of as an abstract opposite to slavery or the

8

tyranny of kings. But this did not rule out the possibility that Frenchmen, and even French kings, might act as liberators rather than tyrants. It was as just such a liberator (from the oath-breaking, misgovernment, and bad laws of King Harold) that William the Conqueror, the first of the French/Norman kings of England, was portrayed following the Conquest of 1066. A century and a half later, greeting an invasion of England led by Louis, the son of the king of France, in the immediate aftermath of Magna Carta, the Anglo-Norman-Welsh writer, Gerald of Wales, proclaimed Louis as yet another French libertator: 'The madness of slavery now ends; times of liberty are granted; English necks are freed from the yoke.' This was a cross-Channel society, a seething coalition of peoples and provinces governed by a cosmopolitan political elite. Whether in any meaningful sense it was a society to which we can apply concepts such as nationhood, let alone statehood, remains a hotly debated topic. Whatever 'national' sentiment existed, the majority of the population – illiterate, bred to the land – served merely as passive and impoverished observers of the politics of the great. This was a chessboard world of kings, bishops, knights, and pawns, and the chessboard has always been a place of supranational, multilingual rivalries.

The dynasty of Henry II owed its rise to Henry's father, Geoffrey Plantagenet, the grandfather of King John, who in the 1120s had married Matilda, widowed daughter of Henry I, King of England, himself the last surviving son of William 'the Conqueror'. When Henry died in 1135, with no direct male heir, Geoffrey, Matilda, and their sons, including the future King Henry II, inherited a claim to the English throne. It was a claim that was bitterly disputed. The Angevins were the traditional arch-enemies of the Normans. Matilda was a woman at a time when succession through the female line was far from universally accepted. In 1135, immediately after Henry I's death, the late King's favourite nephew, Stephen of Blois, moved to seize the treasury and principal cities of England, staging what was in effect a *coup d'état*. Stephen was crowned by the Church. A large number of the barons of England, who had previously sworn oaths to recognize Matilda as heir to the throne, now broke these oaths and proclaimed Stephen as king.

Stephen's was by no means the first such *coup* in English history. At the death of his elder brother, William Rufus, Henry I had seized the late king's treasure, gained control of London, and had himself proclaimed king despite the existence of other claimants. Rufus had himself taken the throne of England despite the claims of his older brother Robert, the Conqueror's eldest son. As this implies, and as a result of the great upheaval of 1066, there was no longer clear consensus as to whether right or might should determine succession to the English throne. Ultimately, God alone could judge the outcome of a succession dispute, as he had judged the Battle of Hastings in 1066, through bloodshed and a great ordeal in arms. So that their seizures of power might be 'justified' (that is to say, cloaked in a largely spurious rhetoric of 'justice'), both Henry I, in 1100, and Stephen, in 1135, issued 'coronation' charters, declaring their intention to rule according to custom and law, repudiating tyranny and deliberately blackening the memory of their immediate predecessors in order to proclaim their own fitness to rule.

Henry I's coronation charter is of particular significance to the story of Magna Carta since it was used as model by the barons of 1215 for the concessions sought from King John. In just over twenty clauses, it spells out Henry I's determination to rule justly. The king would thus 'free' the Church, ending the practice by which Henry's father and brother had collected the revenues of churches between the death of one bishop or abbot and the election of another. All such evil customs would be abolished. The king would reduce his interference in the inheritance and marriage practices of his barons, in effect recognizing his obligation, in accordance with the teachings of Christ and the Gospels, to protect the rights of widows and orphans. Rather than charging a swingeing fine (known as a 'relief') from his barons to inherit their fathers' lands, the king would restrict himself to a 'legitimate and just relief'. Widows would be allowed the lands set aside for them by their husbands or their families (their 'dower' and 'marriage portion'). They would not be forced by the king to remarry against their consent. Those fearing death should be allowed to make wills disposing of personal property. The goods of those who died intestate should be distributed by their families rather than by the king. Those who offended the king should be fined according to the gravity of their offence, rather than risk confiscation of their entire estate. In the case of certain specified royal prerogatives (the king's right to take particular taxes, his collection of debts owed to previous kings, his control over the minting of coin, his right to set aside land as 'forest' or hunting reserves in which neither the animals nor their habitat could be disturbed on pain of drastic punishment), Henry I pledged himself to a degree of moderation. Finally, he agreed to confirm the law of Edward the Confessor (the '*lagam Edwardi regis*') and to abandon anything seized unjustly since King Edward's time, in effect establishing a mythological golden age of justice before 1066 to which the fallen standards of present times might be restored.

During his 35-year reign, Henry I kept virtually none of the promises set out in his coronation charter. The appeal made in 1100 to the past and the good old law was nonetheless powerful. In the much-conquered land of England, as in many societies confronted with fundamental change, custom and tradition became the watchwords of those bewildered by the unpredictability of current affairs. In particular, the law could be seen as embodying fundamental principles, of justice and equity, preserved across even the widest gulfs of conquest and disorder. Edward the Confessor himself, prior to his coronation in 1043, had sworn to uphold the laws of his predecessor, King Cnut, and Cnut, although a Danish usurper, had almost certainly sworn to observe the laws of England after seizing the throne in 1016.

Oath-taking, by kings as by their subjects, was an essential feature of these arrangements. It was for the breaking of their oaths that both King Harold in 1066 and King Stephen after 1135 were stigmatized as tyrants and usurpers. As this in turn suggests, beyond such oaths, there was very little sanction short of rebellion that could be applied to a king who broke his promises. Oath-taking mattered because, in an age without effective sanctions or independent appeals' tribunals, the consequences of oath-breaking could prove disastrous for individuals as for nations.

Although the promises of early kings to uphold the law had not necessarily been set down in writing as 'coronation charters', the written law codes of English kings, from Ethelbert of Kent in the 600s to Ethelred in 1014 and Cnut after 1016, were already associated with the process by which kings were deemed fit to rule. Ethelbert's code, like many of those that followed, was written in the Anglo-Saxon vernacular. As a result, it is to be distinguished from other such codes issued on the continent, most notably from the so-called 'Salic Laws' of the Franks, written in Latin and seeking to imitate Roman imperial practice. Ethelred's code of 1014 invoked nostalgia for the 'good' laws of the past as a model of how kingship itself should operate. All such law codes were intended to give the impression that the king stood at the head of the law, as God's vicar on earth, proclaiming justice for his subjects and issuing laws as both a function and an advertisement of his exalted status.

Once again, there was nothing new in this. The issuing of laws, the deliberate blackening of a predecessor's reputation, and the promise to rule better in future were things already recorded of the Roman emperors, of the kings of Old Testament Judea, and for all we know of the very first rulers to emerge from the prehistoric shades. As long ago as the 6th century BC, the kings of Mesopotamia, the first dynasty to state its claims in something approaching modern writing, had their public monuments carved with inscriptions proclaiming their legitimate right to rule, their descent from kings of the past, and their intention to govern as intermediaries between the realms of heaven and earth. Law and its public proclamation was already a defining feature of civilization. In Homer's *Odyssey*, the greatest of all classical epics, it is not just their consumption of human flesh but their inability to organize public assemblies that marks out the Cyclopedes as beyond the bounds of civilized society, lawless and hence barbaric.

By proclaiming his ability to offer good law, in 1100 Henry I staged a successful bid for the throne of England. Stephen's *coup* of 1135, by contrast, plunged England and Normandy into twenty years of civil war. Arrests at court, the fear of treachery, accusations of betrayal, and the ravaging of rival baronial estates, all served to poison relations among the Anglo-Norman ruling classes, ensuring that the scars of war remained tender long after peace was theoretically restored. In the process, there was a bruising, though still hotly debated, lurch in the balance between royal and baronial power.

England was a much governed land, since long before 1066 divided into shires and hundreds, accustomed to traditions of central and local government in which the king's authority, communicated by written instructions ('writs') dispatched to sheriffs and other local officials, commanded at least superficial assent. This system had survived the Norman Conquest of 1066, albeit overlaid now by a tradition of 'feudalism' in which, as a result of conquest, all land was supposed to belong ultimately to the king and hence could be offered by the king to his faithful supporters in return for homage and service in the king's armies. Those holding their lands directly from the king, known as barons or 'tenants in chief', used their landed resources to reward their own followers, establishing a distribution of the property of England in which a small elite, composed of knights holding land from barons, and barons holding their land directly from the king, lorded it over the vast majority of the population, itself divided between freemen, able to marry or go where they pleased, and serfs, generally bonded to their land, unfree, unable to marry without purchasing their lord's permission. Historians today shun the word 'feudalism', invented in the 18th century as a pejorative term to describe the lordly exploitation of the lower classes that characterized pre-Revolutionary France or Russia. Nonetheless, 'feudalism' remains a word that, if it did not exist, we would find it necessary to invent.

Many of the practices described in Henry I's coronation charter, and later in Magna Carta, were the consequences of that 'feudalism' introduced by the Norman Conquest. As a result of 1066, all barons in England were deemed to hold their lands from the king, a situation that had not prevailed, or at least whose precise terms had never been so clearly defined under Anglo-Saxon rule. The king as overlord acquired a series of lordly privileges that historians sometimes refer to as 'feudal incidents' (the 'incidental' consequences of lordship). These included jurisdiction over widows and orphans, and the right to demand particular payments resulting from the baronial life cycle: at inheritance and succession, at marriage and at death. In theory, since all land was held from the king, the king might deprive a baron's son of the right to succeed to his father's lands. This, however, was a drastic step, generally only taken in cases of outright idiocy or rebellion.

Rather like the powers of the modern British Parliament (which in the standard theoretical formulation can do anything save turn a man into a woman or a woman into a man – a statement which itself may need recasting in light of recent medical procedures), the authority of a medieval king was vaster in theory than in any practice that a king would dare attempt. From at least the 1140s, indeed probably since the 1070s, it was accepted tradition that land passed from father to son without arbitrary intervention from the king. Nonetheless, if there were any hitch in this pattern – if, for example, a baron died leaving female heirs or grandchildren or only nephews, or if the land, for want of a direct heir, 'escheated' (that is, returned to the king as overlord) – then it was the king's will that determined what would happen next. In these circumstances, royal favour had to be bid for and bought by whichever potential heir had the deeper pockets. At times of crisis or uncertainty, or when the king himself faced particular financial pressures, 'feudal incidents' could become a major source of tension between the king and the political elite.

The Norman kings, like their Anglo-Saxon predecessors, made laws that they expected to be obeyed throughout their realm. Such laws were not so comprehensive as to govern all disputes or eventualities. A large part of criminal jurisdiction, as of the resolution of quarrels over land or property, remained a local affair, very much a question of self-help by those for whom feuding was a common pastime and for whom might was a great deal more apparent in their daily lives than any sort of abstract right. Presented as semi-official law collections attributed to 'good' rulers of the past, in particular to kings Cnut, Edward the Confessor, William I and Henry I, a series of manuscripts circulated in 12th-century England purporting to set out the particular codes of law that these kings had issued. Many were founded upon wishful thinking and the attribution to previous kings of laws that 'ought' to have been upheld but which rarely were. None can be considered a comprehensive statement of past, let alone of present, law. The courts themselves were governed first and foremost by the king and his whims, and thereafter by custom and by communal memory. Nowhere was there anything like today's Statute Book or Law Reports from which lawyers, litigants, and the public at large could learn the exact condition and letter of the law.

One of the most influential guidebooks to legal procedure written at this time, *On the Laws and Customs of the Realm of England*, attributed to Ranulf de Glanville, Henry II's chief legal officer of the 1170s and 1180s, begins with a claim both that 'English laws are unwritten' and that 'it is utterly impossible for the laws and rules (*leges…et iura*) of the realm to be reduced to writing'. For this, Glanville blamed the sheer profusion of laws, and the ignorance of those who might write them down. Hence the insistence by later legal historians that the 'Common Law' of England was a matter of precedent and the slow evolution of custom derived from a multitude of individual cases: case law, not statute law. This is a potentially misleading statement since there were statutes in plenty. What there was not was any systematic codification of these statutes into a definitive statement of English 'Law'. To this extent, the 'Common Law' of England has to be distinguished from other legal systems, most notably from Roman civil law, still in the 12th century enormously influential in southern Europe, codified and collected as long ago as the 6th century by the Emperor Justinian, and thereafter circulating throughout the Middle Ages as the so-called *Corpus Iuris Civilis*. In the same way, by the 1160s, the laws of the Church, so-called 'Canon Law', although governed by a multitude of precedents rather than by simple statute, had been systematically digested into textbooks, most notably the *Decretum* of the Italian lawyer Gratian, in which were organized many hundreds of the individual papal letters (or 'decretals') in which the law of the Church was set out.

Since Glanville's text takes the form of a commentary on legal procedure, explaining the use and meaning of the dozens of individual 'writs' through which the king controlled the activities of his courts, even after Glanville there was nothing that could be considered an officially sanctioned collection of English statutes. The earliest books of statutes in this sense date from the late 13th century and even then recite only the most recent of royal legislation, not the great bulk of customary law which such legislation was intended to adjust. Nonetheless, the willingness of 12th-century collectors to compile legal manuscripts in which Anglo-Saxon and later laws were presented in coherent series, for example in the great book of precedents compiled for the bishops of Rochester in the 1120s (the so-called *Textus Roffensis*) in which the coronation charter of Henry I was inserted as if it were merely the latest in a series of statutes stretching back to the 7th-century Anglo-Saxon law code of king Ethelbert of kent (d. 616), testifies to a desire to find in the law not only practical measures for the regulation of crime or the rights of property but a semi-divine tradition, hallowed by antiquity, in which the rulings of modern kings could be seen to stand in direct relation to the law codes of their ancestors. Those ancestral codes in turn stood in sequence with the books of law bequeathed to Old Testament kings of Judea by Moses, the prophets, and ultimately by God.

In all of this, the maintenance of public peace and the administration of what might be considered justice remained essential attributes of kingship. From the king's point of view, the administration of justice not only advertised his authority but supplied substantial profits in the form of fines made in his courts, bribes paid for the doing of justice, and all of the other means by which the machinery of the law was oiled and made to run smoothly. Once again, as expressed in the opening sentences of Glanville's treatise *On the Laws*, written in praise of King Henry II, the father of King John:

> Not only must royal power be supplied with arms against rebels and peoples who rise up against king and realm, but it is fitting that such power be adorned with laws for ruling peaceful and subject peoples.

We should not exaggerate the degree to which England was centrally governed, either before or after 1066. The Anglo-Saxon law codes were to a large extent intended not to assume full royal administration of the law but merely to place the king at the head of the law-making process. What was at stake here was the regulation of what remained essentially private feuding, with the king and his advisors merely establishing a tariff of payments (*wergild*) to be paid to the victims of crime or their kin. Ethelbert's code, for example, reads for the most part rather like the small print to a modern personal-injury insurance policy: 'For the four front teeth, six shillings each; for the tooth that comes next, four shillings, that which comes next, three shillings', and so on through a bewildering array of the potential consequences of inter-personal violence.

Just as the king did not claim to administer, merely to regulate, these processes, so there was much that went on in the shires that was not controlled from the centre. In the absence of any effective police force (an absence not effectively remedied until the late 19th century), self help remained the principal means to secure justice or right. Even the sheriff, the king's principal local officer, depended upon hired muscle (the serjeants of the peace) and the raising of a county 'posse' (literally, a bunch of 'can-doers') when called upon to deal with the more severe forms of lawlessness. This was a world closer to that of the Wild West and the lynch mob than to Scotland Yard. As late as 1221, for example, a criminal convicted in the king's courts in Gloucestershire was sentenced to blinding and castration at the hands of his victim's family, the young men hurling his testicles around in a brutally staged act of vengeance.

Even the Church, for all its commitment to peace, offered a system of law and discipline that was far from entirely centralized or universal. The great chapter houses of the English cathedrals or monasteries, in each of which the canons or monks met daily to discuss their business and to administer the laws of their community, demonstrate that communal decision-making and debates over justice were endemic to medieval society. Yet even these 'chapters' remained intensely localized affairs. England was a land of many hundreds or even thousands of interlocking jurisdictions, each of them jealously guarded against intrusion by its neighbours. For a modern equivalent, we might look to the colleges of Oxford or Cambridge, all of them subjected by common imperatives to the rule of a 'university', separated from one another by only a few yards of wall or parapet, yet still individually governed by a hundred or more independent 'governing bodies', each with its own particular statutes and customs.

As a unifying and governing principle over and above such diversity, the image of a king ruling by justice and the law remained a powerful one. Above all, the imperative to maintain peace, to allow the king to impose such peace, and hence not to impede his officials or messengers in the discharge of their duties, gained powerful currency. The king stood above the law, or at least above all human laws below those decreed by God. Once again to quote Glanville, himself quoting a famous tag from Roman law, 'What pleases the prince has the force of law'. A king's subjects, by contrast, were precisely that: 'subjected' to the laws that the king made or interpreted and to the peace that the king sought to maintain.

In the 1140s, as a result of King Stephen's seizure of power, this entire tradition juddered to a standstill. The king's peace was shattered. Injustice went unpunished. The unjust enjoyed public reward. The criminal activities of barons or mercenaries were placed beyond the reach of the king's officers or courts. Even such longstanding symbols of central government as a single silver coinage, stamped with the king's crowned image, ubiquitous in England since the time of King Edgar in the 970s, were challenged as rival barons minted their own coins, established their own local alliances, and administered their own rough justice, virtually irrespective of command either from Stephen or from the party of Matilda. Having been steered towards centralization and strong royal authority by the first three of its Anglo-Norman kings, England slipped backwards towards baronial self-help and regional power struggles.

It used to be asserted that Stephen's reign witnessed 'anarchy'. It is now generally agreed that this is to exaggerate the degree of disorder. In the regions of England closest to his capital city of London, Stephen commanded considerable authority. Taxes continued to be raised to pay the costs of war. In political terms, nonetheless, the outcome was a stalemate resolved only in the 1150s when Henry Plantagenet, son and heir to Geoffrey and

Matilda, reached a compromise with Stephen, itself brokered via barons and churchmen acting in the mutual self-interest of the realm. In 1153, a treaty was negotiated in which Henry recognized Stephen's right to rule. In return, Stephen recognized Henry as his successor to the throne. Once again, setting significant precedents for the events of King John's reign, the treaty of 1153, like the coronation charters of Henry I and Stephen, was negotiated under the auspices of the English Church. It was not only proclaimed in the English localities but entrusted for safe-keeping, as a written peace 'treaty', to various of the greater ecclesiastical archives, most notably those of the archbishop of Canterbury. The Church had emerged, as long ago as the 7th or 8th century, as one of the chief guardians not only of public peace but of the documentary evidences by which such peace was proclaimed. It now played a leading role in broadcasting the king's peace, through arbitration resolving political disputes to the mutual benefit of all.

Chapter 2

Angevin kingship: making and breaking royal law

King Stephen died within ten months of the proclamation of his peace. In 1154, Henry Plantagenet found himself not only heir to his father's estates in Anjou and to the conquered duchy of Normandy but to the throne of England once held by his grandfather, King Henry I. At or shortly after his coronation, he issued yet another 'coronation charter', a brief statement addressed to his earls, barons, and faithful subjects, sealed with his royal seal, notifying them of his determination, 'for the common interest and improvement of my whole realm', to restore to God, the Church, and all his earls, barons, and men all gifts, liberties, and free customs granted by King Henry I, repudiating all evil customs that Henry I had repudiated. The idea of a community, of the realm, and of the common interests of the English people was already an ancient one. In 1154, it was once again advertised as something under the particular protection of the Church and king. The king recognized no superior authority. He was placed on earth as God's vicar. But in his actions, he necessarily had to promote the common interests of his realm in accordance with the Church's teachings.

By the time of the establishment of the Plantagenet dynasty on the throne of England, a number of principles vital to the future issue of Magna Carta had already been agreed: recognition of a code of laws whether written or, more often, customary and unwritten; the issuing of promises by the king to uphold such laws and to recognize the liberties of his subjects; and a role for the Church in negotiating and broadcasting such promises. Far from being a unique or entirely novel statement of principles, Magna Carta was merely the latest in a series of such charters issued by the kings of England to their subjects in the years before 1154, intended to advertise the king's virtue, to promote peace, and to re-establish harmony between king and community. What was unusual about Magna Carta was first and foremost its size and the detail with which it sought to regulate the king's dealings. Secondly, it followed after a great hiatus in English politics, between 1154 and 1215, when Henry II and his Plantagenet successors issued no further coronation charters and threatened fundamentally to destabilize the relationship between king and people. This destabilization was itself the product of the particular pressures under which Henry II and his successors were placed.

Henry himself was heir to the rulers of England, Normandy, and Anjou. Through a marriage hastily negotiated in 1152 to the recently divorced wife of the King of France, Eleanor of Aquitaine, Henry found himself as *de facto* ruler of a vast swathe of territory extending from his father's lands on the Loire as far south as Bordeaux and the badlands of the French south-west. Through a combination of fortuitous circumstance and dynastic accident, Henry became ruler of an 'empire' that extended from the Cheviots in the far north of England to the Pyrenees on the frontiers with Spain. His was the greatest territorial lordship in France, and one of the greatest in western Europe, amassed since the reign of the Emperor Charlemagne more than three centuries before.

Two imperatives henceforth dominated Henry II's reign: the need to restore public order and royal authority in an England recently ravaged by civil war, and the need to defend his vast French territories from the threat posed by his principal rival, Louis VII,

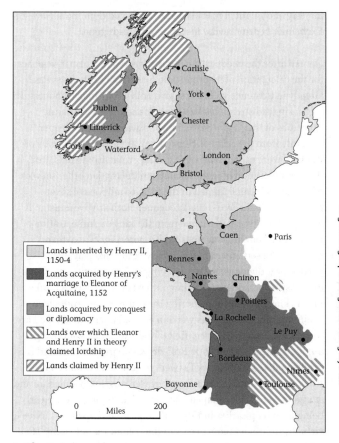

2. The Angevin empire

the Capetian King of France. In both of these objectives, Henry was broadly successful. In both, silver was the principal fuel of his success. His great wealth, particularly the wealth derived from the much-governed and hence much-taxed realm of England, enabled him to pay for armies and castles with which to defend his lordships in France. It also paid for the public display of his majesty and might across his widely scattered dominion. Here, the Exchequer became a vital instrument of his regime.

Named after the chequered cloth that served as a primitive abacus for the calculation of its profits and losses, the Exchequer was already in existence within fifty years of the Norman Conquest. Its origins indeed stretch back to the remarkable tax-gathering capacities of the Anglo-Saxon kings. It was to the Exchequer, certainly from the reign of Henry I onwards, that the sheriffs of England were called to account for the profits from lands, from the administration of justice, and from the myriad other sources of the king's income tapped in the form of millions of silver pennies now paid across the Exchequer cloth at Westminster. A large part of this income came from the king's administration of justice and from judicial 'fines' and 'amercements': payments made for the settlement of disputes, charges made against particular individuals for wrongdoing or for incurring the king's displeasure, on occasion shading into what were in effect bribes for the king's favour in furthering the cause of one landholder against another. Such fines were an age-old phenomenon and are recorded as early as the very first of the Exchequer's surviving accounts, the so-called 'Pipe Roll' drawn up in 1130 to record the profits and losses of Henry I's twenty-ninth year. Similar Pipe Rolls (named from the fact that they were originally rolled up and stored in a container shaped like a length of piping) were clearly being drawn up earlier in Henry I's reign, and thereafter survive in virtually unbroken sequence from the second year of Henry II, 1155–6, through to the 1830s when the Whig administration elected in the aftermath of the Great Reform Act cleared away at least part of the clutter and sinecurism inherited from the medieval past.

Precisely because they are mere lists of profits and losses, untinged by the rhetoric or exaggeration that casts the opinions of the chroniclers into suspicion, the Pipe Rolls reveal more clearly than any other source the extent to which the government of Henry II and his sons was founded upon extortion and the use of 'justice' as a tool not of abstract right but of royal policy. In a situation, after 1154, in which the legacy of Stephen's reign ensured that there were very frequently two or more barons laying claim to a single estate, the opportunities for the king to profit were irresistible. Courtiers shared in this bounty. But they too were ultimately subject to royal whim, caught up in the rise and inevitable fall of the great wheel of fortune. A few examples must suffice. Robert Belet, the king's hereditary butler, was accused of insolence in denying the king a gift of a sparrowhawk. He was forced to buy back royal favour through a fine of £100, imposed in 1165, still being paid eighteen years later and involving the loss of a significant portion of his lands. Henry of Essex, the king's constable and heir to one of the few Anglo-Saxon landholders to have weathered the storms of the Norman Conquest, was accused of cowardice in dropping the king's banner during Henry II's Welsh expedition of 1157. He was forced to undergo an 'ordeal', in a trial by battle against his chief accuser. Henry lost the fight and was left for dead, an object lesson in how God himself could ultimately judge the right or wrong of any dispute. His lands were confiscated by the king.

Such drastic declines in fortune were comparatively rare during the reign of Henry II: most of those who prospered at Henry's court were permitted, albeit with an imminent sense of fear and foreboding, to reap the harvest of their prosperity. Even so, the most dramatic of all the incidents of Henry's reign, the king's great falling-out with his former chancellor, Thomas Becket, can be seen as yet another outcome of the arbitrary and uneasy nature of the king's favour. Becket, once the king's boon companion, elected archbishop of Canterbury as a direct result of the king's friendship, refused as archbishop to do the king's bidding. The outcome was a state trial at the Council of Northampton in 1164. Becket was called to account for all of the profits that he had made as the king's favourite. He instead sought exile overseas: an exile that ended six years later with his dramatic return to Canterbury and his no less dramatic murder on the flagstones of his own cathedral church.

In all of this, the Exchequer at Westminster, joined from the 1170s by similar Exchequers for both Normandy and Ireland, presided over the manoeuvring of royal finance, with the king and his needs arbitrarily trumping the moves of all other players. Using the financial resources which the Exchequer bestowed, and with his sons and daughters serving as pawns in a game of dynastic chess, Henry forged alliances with the ruling families of Germany, Sicily, Spain, and France. With the king of France branded an incompetent in military affairs, Henry extended his authority inland along the valley of the River Seine to within only twenty or thirty miles of Paris. Paris indeed became a frontier city, supreme as a centre of learning and culture yet perilously encircled by the great power blocks ruled by the kings of England in Normandy, the counts of Flanders north of the Seine, and the counts of Blois-Champagne to the south and east. Meanwhile, having seized back Northumberland and Cumbria from the king of Scots, in 1172 Henry fulfilled a long-term ambition to carry his lordship into Ireland, intervening in what had previously been private warfare led by Anglo-Norman mercenaries to declare himself ruler of Dublin and the south-eastern regions of Leinster and Meath. All of these conquests and consolidations were financed from the profits of lordship and war, above all from the rich resources of England and the English crown.

The literary monuments left behind by Henry's court are every bit as extraordinary as the extent of his 'empire'. Not since Charlemagne could one ruler claim to have presided over so rich an assembly of written memorials. The chronicles of Roger of Howden or Ralph of Diss; the treatise on government (the *Policraticus*) composed by John of Salisbury; the letter collections of Peter of Blois; the treatise on the king's finances (the so-called *Dialogue of the Exchequer*) written by Henry II's treasurer, Richard fitz Nigel; the collection of tall stories composed for the court's entertainment by Walter Map; the book on manners and deportment written by Stephen of Fougères, a former servant of the king's chancery – all of these books and much else besides testify to a determination to memorialize the court of Henry II unrivalled by any other court of 12th-century Europe. What is remarkable about these writings is not just their range and richness but the fact that, in the very act of celebrating the court, they express such biting criticisms of king and courtiers alike. Far removed from the sycophantic literature sponsored by the Capetian kings of France, Plantagenet court writers encouraged a view of Plantagenet government that was as sinister as it was magnificent.

Behind this lay two perceptions. The first, a prejudice age old and already familiar from the writing of Roman authors, most notably from Suetonius's biographies of the first *Twelve Caesars*, was that the new imperial dynasty of Henry II was itself an unstable and parvenu phenomenon, risen from the dust by accident and circumstance to only brief supremacy over human affairs. Not just secular philosophers but the Church taught that royal authority was something inherently fleeting and untrustworthy. The Bible was as full of bad as of good kings. Against every Solomon or David could be raised an example of a tyrant, whether a foreigner such as Pharaoh or an Israelite such as Herod. Although dressed and crowned as kings, the Plantagenets were perceived as having set themselves up as vain yet unworthy challengers to the supremacy of God.

It was this irrationality, instability, and unpredictability of Plantagenet kingship that emerged as a principal theme in criticism of the Plantagenet court. The image, for example, derived from the letters of John of Salisbury, of Henry II so 'aflame with his usual rage, (that) he tore his hat from his head, undid his belt... tore the silken covering from his bed, and began to eat the straw on the floor, as if he were sitting in a ditch'; the tradition that the Plantagenets were themselves descended from a she-devil, Melusine, half-woman half-serpent, reported as early as the 1150s in a remark attributed to St Bernard ('From the Devil they came, and to the Devil they will undoubtedly return'); the idea, to be found in anecdotes recorded by Walter Map or Peter of Blois, that the Plantagenet court was heir to the pursuits of the mythical huntsman, king Herlequin, doomed to wander the earth from region to region like demons of the underworld, dining by candlelight rather than by the natural light of day; the very idea of hunting as a defining feature of court culture, of the deliberate and ritualized shedding of blood as an action appropriate to a king whose justice on occasion required the pronunciation of sentence of death – all of this speaks of a kingship that was far from universally admired.

The authority exercised by the Plantagenets was subject to particular as well as to generic criticim. Henry II might be perceived as a powerful ruler whose authority traversed the English Channel, but his power was itself tarnished by rumours of violence, lust, and avarice. The greatest of Henry's crimes, overshadowing all others, was his involvement in the murder of his own archbishop, Thomas Becket, struck down in Canterbury Cathedral in 1170. Henry II did not directly order the murder of Thomas Becket. But he could not escape the charge that his anger had provoked the deed. Becket's dispute with the crown had begun with personalities rather than ideology, as the outcome of friendship networks turned poisonously sour. Yet its startling climax, the murder in the cathedral, and the recognition throughout Christendom that Becket had died as a saint and martyr, victim to the violence provoked by an angry king, lent a wholly new slant to criticisms of Henry II and his dynasty. Henceforth, the Plantagenets could never entirely escape the perception that they were, of their essence, a family of bloodshed and impiety.

As if it were a direct result of the king's loss of God's favour, Becket's murder was followed within a matter of only three years by an eruption of violence within the Plantagenet family itself. In

1173, Henry II's wife and at least three of their sons joined in rebellion with the kings of France and Scotland. Earls and barons who had resented the past twenty years of Henry II's ascendancy, but who had remained powerless to oppose it, now rose to support the rebellion of the king's sons. Local grievances, allowed to lie dormant since the reign of Stephen, were once again voiced. Old wounds were re-opened. The chaos of Stephen's reign seemed about to be revisited. In all of this, the perception that the king had broken faith with the Church and that God would condone the humiliation of a king who had himself condoned the murder of St Thomas Becket played no small part.

Yet, in the outcome, it was not the rebels but the king who triumphed. By Christmas 1174, Henry II was once again in full command of his family and his lands. Where previously he had controlled a minority of England's castles, he now seized so many from the rebels of 1173–4 that never again was he to have control of anything other than a majority. Fines imposed at the Exchequer in the 1150s or 1160s and set for payment over many years or decades were now rescheduled for immediate collection. The Exchequer functioned here as a tool of arbitrary royal power. Where, in the 1160s, the business of the king's courts had begun to expand, to allow for new processes in the administration of justice and the settlement of disputes over land, after 1174 the floodgates opened to admit a vast increase in the business, both civil and criminal, that the royal law courts now handled.

It is in this period that historians have sought to place the emergence of the English 'Common Law': a system based upon custom and precedent, governed by procedures themselves initiated by writs or letters of instruction obtainable from the king or his chief law officers. Although the roots of this system stretched back into the Anglo-Saxon law codes by which legal custom had first been clarified and codified, its precise procedures are first described in detail in the treatise attributed to Glanville composed in the 1180s. This was a system of law subject to the king, that could ultimately be subverted or overturned should the king decide either to delay or to deny what might otherwise be agreed was 'justice'. Delay was one of the principal techniques of Angevin government. Indeed, Henry II is said to have been instructed by his own mother, the Empress Matilda, that it was better that the king withhold final judgment and fail to bring resolution to a dispute if, by this means, both parties could be persuaded that it was in their best interests to buy the king's friendship. The idea that the king should set down what was just or customary in the form of written laws, governing not just his subjects but the king himself, was not an innovation of Henry II's reign, let alone of the period after the failed rebellion of 1174. Even so, it was during this same period that chroniclers, most notably the Yorkshireman Roger of Howden, himself a minor official in Henry II's service, first began to record the texts of specific 'assizes', or laws emanating from the king.

Under Henry II, there was a very considerable increase in the jurisdiction of the king's courts and in the degree to which they were staffed by legally trained, semi-professional judges competent to administer justice both over property and over crime. An increase in the supply of the procedures of justice met an increase in popular demand for justice to be done. Whether supply or demand was the motive force here remains one of the more significant debating points for historians inclined to view these developments as an extension of the jurisdictional powers of the crown rather than of abstract 'justice'. What is not in doubt is that queues of litigants emerged, eager to bring their disputes for the king to settle. New written instruments, the so-called 'Final Concords' setting out, in semi-official and self-consciously 'legalistic' Latin the terms of court settlements, the king's assizes, and, from the 1180s onwards, the very court reports that the justices had drafted (the so-called 'rolls' of the justices), begin to survive in ever increasing numbers. Roger of Howden, moving in court circles, was in a position to acquire copies of half a dozen of the king's assizes henceforth preserved in his chronicle. This is a pathetic rate of survival for the king's laws, at least when compared with later times. For example, two of the most important of Henry II's assizes, introduced in the 1160s and intended to provide speedy redress for large numbers of litigants seeking the restoration of property claimed by direct inheritance ('mort d'ancestor') or from which they could show they had been recently ejected ('new seizures', hence 'the assize of novel disseisin'), are known only from their effects and their later acceptance as standard procedures in English law. The texts of these assizes, the law or 'statutes' by which they were proclaimed, have been entirely lost. Even so, the 'Assize of Clarendon' of 1166 and its successors, preserved by Howden, are the first official codifications of law into statute form to survive in England since the Laws of Cnut issued in the 1020s.

The 'Assize of Clarendon' was an attempt by Henry II to control (or at least to be seen attempting to control) crime, to punish robbery and murder, to ensure that gaols were maintained in each county town, to deter vagrancy, and to ensure that all lived, to some extent, under the watch of neighbours or lords willing to vouch for their good conduct. Ironically (and somewhat confusingly), the 'Assize of Clarendon' followed only three years after another written text, the so-called 'Constitutions of Clarendon', proclaimed at the same royal hunting lodge at Clarendon in Wiltshire, in the case of the 'Constitutions' as an attempt to set out in writing the extent to which the English Church should be subordinate to the king. It was the 'Constitutions of Clarendon', and their repudiation by the Church, that served as one of the principal rallying cries in Henry II's dispute with Thomas Becket. What was remarkable about the 'Constitutions' was not that they were asserted – kings had traditionally exercised considerable authority over the day-to-day government, office-holding, and resolution of disputes within the Church – but that they were reduced to writing. England and England's kings were entering a new age in which law and custom were increasingly to be regarded not as immemorial traditions committed to the memories of the older and more respectable members of the community, but as 'laws' in the modern sense, issued as written decrees. By issuing his laws for the Church in the form of the highly controversial Constitutions of Clarendon, Henry II set a precedent for other sorts of written law, not least for Magna Carta, seeking not to license but to the curb the arbitrary exercise of royal power.

The Assize of Clarendon, like the subsequent Assize of Northampton, is a text principally concerned with the king's role as protector of his people and hence with the obligations of local lords and officials rather than with any greater abstractions or legal principles. It envisages a situation in which a great deal of law continued to be a matter of self-help, and in particular a situation in which the detection and punishment of criminals remained an *ad hoc* affair, brutally administered through trial by battle or the digging of ordeal pits and the subjection of those accused to ritual submersion in water or the carrying of red-hot irons to prove or disprove their guilt. Nonetheless, from the 1160s, we can already point to a body of statutory laws issued by the king, proclaimed in the king's courts, above all in the county courts of the various English shires. Such laws were composed in abrupt yet precise Latin phrases, themselves owing something to the longstanding tradition of Anglo-Saxon law-making, something also to the wider European tradition of laws made both by the Roman emperors of antiquity (reported in the so-called *Corpus Iuris Civilis*) and by popes and churchmen as reported in the various digests of Canon Law.

Henry II's legal reforms themselves had little to do with a search for abstract ideas of right or equity. They speak instead of the determination to employ law as a symbol and instrument of royal authority. In particular, law would be used to heal the wounds of the 1140s and to re-establish royal control over property disputes that during Stephen's reign had been determined not by the king but by inter-baronial feuding. Law would also encourage large numbers of litigants, ranging from barons to priests and from the higher aristocracy all the way down to peasants owning a few acres of land, to settle their disputes in royal rather than in private baronial courts. Cases that might previously have been heard in the lord's manor court, or before the lord himself, were now diverted, thanks to the king's new legal procedures, to be settled in the courts of the king. Thanks to the considerable increase in their business, the king's courts began to expand both in competence and in the frequency and bureaucratic uniformity of their meetings. Some cases continued to be brought before the king in person (to the court 'coram rege'). More often, however, litigants appeared before the king's justices and officials, sometimes in the Exchequer, but increasingly in the *ad hoc* sessions held before groups of Exchequer and other royal officials now known from their place of meeting in Westminster Hall as 'The Bench', subsequently described as the 'Court of Common Pleas'. To ensure that criminals detained in local gaols were brought to justice, and to deal with the backlog of property and other disputes in the shires, from the 1160s regular judicial visitations of England were organized, known as 'eyres', in which the king's justices, and considerable numbers of the king's friends drafted in according to need, served as judges travelling in circuit from shire to shire. Perhaps as early as the 1150s, other 'eyres' were convened to deal with justice within the forests: parts of England, at their fullest extent covering nearly one-third of the country, where the game was to be preserved for the king's hunting, and where particularly brutal punishments – maiming and ultimately death – had been introduced to penalize those who trespassed either against the game (the 'venison') or the 'vert' (the natural habitat in which game was preserved).

To meet the needs of this new world of law and lawyers, the king's justices, originally recruited from amongst the ranks of the sheriffs, Exchequer officials, or courtiers, became increasingly specialized professionals, learned in the law and dealing for most of their careers with matters of justice rather than with more general duties to the king. To represent litigants in court, and to guard against the expensive consequences of incompetent pleading, a distinct body of legal experts emerged, offering professional counsel to those pleading in court. From these developments emerged those representative figures, the judges standing in place of the king, and the attorneys standing in place of their clients, who today still embody the traditions of English law. The emergence of the legal profession was itself to a large extent a consequence of the reforms of Henry II.

Besides boosting the image and majesty of the king, Henry II's reforms supplied a very practical boost to the king's finances. Court fees and not so officially sanctioned bribes now swelled the king's coffers. Fines and 'amercements' paid for settlements, for mispleading in court, or for failure to attend court hearings, money offered behind the scenes to speed procedures or to ensure a successful outcome for one party or another, had long been an occasional profit of lordship. As early as 1130, when the earliest surviving Exchequer Pipe Roll allows us our first glimpse of the king's income, the profits of justice were already a major source of royal wealth. Since a large part of this business was unofficial, concealed in the shadows in which bribery and peculation flourished, we can assume that even the very considerable legal profits revealed from the Pipe Rolls represent only the tip of a far larger iceberg. From the 1160s onwards, these profits soared, far outstripping the additional costs of reorganizing the courts. The justices themselves could expect rich pickings, not so much through official salaries or retainers, but from the backstairs intrigue, the bribes, the offerings of food and drink and other inducements that were made by litigants keen to buy a favourable hearing. As new legal remedies were devised, and as increasing numbers of litigants were encouraged to plead in the king's rather than in private courts, so the principles of supply and demand came to apply as much to the law as to any other aspect of the economy. By the 1190s, it was difficult for anyone above the level of the humblest peasant to avoid a regular haemorrhage of amercements and fees paid for actions in court. By the same token, there were remarkably few English property-holders who were not made regularly and personally familiar with the procedures of the king's courts.

From the king's courts came an image of the king as God's vicar on earth, a sense that the king himself stood in judgment above the petty disputes of his subjects and a regular stream of income from fines, bribes, and payments for justice. The great legal 'revolution' of Henry II's reign, sometimes described (in hyperbolic terms, since law itself was born long before this) as the 'Birth' of the Common Law, was intended to support strong kingship, not in any way to act as a brake upon the king's sovereign authority. Law, indeed, tended to bolster Plantagenet 'tyranny' just as much as it protected the rights of individual subjects against interference by overmighty kings. Litigants, jurors, and local landholders, though they became increasingly familiar with the king's courts, were at the same time made aware that the king himself claimed to stand above the legal procedures and obligations enforced on his subjects. The great Angevin 'legal leap forwards' reinforced ideas of the king's sovereignty, but only at the expense of advertising the king's own essential immunity from justice or prosecution. The more royal government came to depend upon the law for its income and self-image, the more the king's subjects were likely to resent the king's own apparent disrespect for the laws that he claimed to administer. To this extent, in the very success of Henry II's legal reforms were planted the seeds from which grew that bridling and restraint upon royal power embodied in Magna Carta. Issued almost exactly sixty years after the proclamation of Henry II's first assizes, Magna Carta can be seen as an attempt to bring the king himself within the legal restraints that, from the 1160s onwards, King Henry II and his sons had sought to impose upon their subjects.

Chapter 3
King John's 'little ways'

Magna Carta was a response not to one particular king or set of circumstances, but to an entire tradition of 'Angevin' kingship. There is no doubt that John was a bad king. His badness, however, was an inherited, family characteristic. In many ways, it was his failure to do bad as successfully and with such impunity as either his father or his elder brother that led him to the surrenders that Magna Carta embodied. Henry II had connived at the murder of a sainted archbishop of Canterbury, and had set his own family against him, through adultery, through neglect, and through a refusal to grant his sons the titles and recognitions that they believed to be their due. His eldest son and heir, Richard I, came to the throne in 1189 in the midst of a rebellion against his father, supported by the French. Far from resolving the problems inherent in Plantagenet government, Richard had embarked almost immediately for Crusade, strutting and posing on an international stage yet leaving England in the hands of an administration that soon collapsed into backbiting and chaos. Even so, neither Henry nor Richard faced the disasters that threatened to engulf King John. John's faults were inherited. His failures were his own.

The youngest of Henry II's sons, originally intended for a clerical career, John had been plucked from obscurity at the death of the eldest of his brothers in 1183. Promoted to rule the remotest of

Henry II's dominions, in Ireland, during a brief visit in 1185, he infuriated local opinion through his cruel sense of humour, pulling the long red beards of the Irish kings who came to render homage. In 1189, in secret and apparently at the last moment, he had joined the rebellion of his brother Richard. The news that John's name headed the list of rebels is said to have sent Henry II broken-hearted to his grave. With his father dead and Richard about to embark for Crusade, John was granted an estate out of all proportion to his merits: to Ireland were now added the westernmost counties of England including the port of Bristol, the 'honour of Lancaster', and the so-called 'honour of Mortain' controlling south-western Normandy. Taken as a whole, this was a remarkable collection of lands, a maritime empire linked by the sea from the frontiers of Brittany via the Devon and Dorset coasts to Bristol, Ireland, and the ports of Lancashire. It is perhaps not surprising that one of John's few achievements generally acknowledged is his role in re-establishing England's naval forces, once amongst the glories of Anglo-Saxon England, now revived through John's equipping of a fleet of galleys and his subsequent focus upon Portsmouth as a centre of naval activity. There was only one proviso to Richard's recognition of John's vast estate: John himself was to stay out of England for so long as Richard remained on Crusade.

Typically, John broke his oath almost as soon as Richard had set sail for the East. In particular, he encouraged two lines of attacks against the bitterly divided administration that Richard had left to govern England. Both of them were attacks that were to have a bitter posterity for John himself. In the first place, he and his propagandists criticized the alien birth of William Longchamps, the man whom Richard had left to rule England as justiciar. According to John's supporters, Longchamps was a Frenchman insensitive to English traditions of liberty. Secondly, and despite the fact that the realm was in theory placed under the protection of the Church, at peace during the absence of its king doing God's work in the East, John entered into a treaty with the French king,

Philip Augustus, intending to carve up Richard's lands in northern France. The political crisis that ensued – the worst in English history since Stephen's reign – was exacerbated by the fact that Richard, largely through his own pride and pig-headedness, was captured on his return from the Holy Land, held ransom in Germany for the massive sum of £66,000. The money was raised. England was an immensely wealthy realm. Nonetheless, the pressures brought to bear on the king's finances began to mount.

This was a period of monetary inflation. Since the king's income depended upon resources leased out to the king's sheriffs and other local officers at fixed annual 'farms', inflation posed a particular problem to the royal purse. Where barons and bishops could react to inflationary pressures by taking back the majority of their resources into direct 'demesne' management, thereby avoiding the erosion of their 'farms', the king had other factors to consider. On occasion, he might impose 'increments', additional payments, over and above the traditional farms, but these were locally unpopular. He also had to consider the needs of his sheriffs. The sheriffs took their profit from the difference between what they collected for the king and the 'farm' that they were obliged to pay each year at the Exchequer. As farms remained static but income rose, the sheriffs' profits mounted, so that more and more income was diverted from the king himself to his local henchmen. This, however, was the price that the king had to pay for recruiting major figures to serve as his enforcers in the shires. If he raised the sheriffs' farms or sought to abandon 'farms' altogether by paying fixed salaries to sheriffs thereafter expected to account to the Exchequer for all their revenues, the effect would be to discourage great men from taking up office as sheriff. The king would lose in political credibility what he gained in hard cash.

Both inflation and the cost of Richard's ransom were to have long-term effects. For perhaps the first time since the tenth century, we find England's kings struggling to pay their way. A pattern was established whereby the king found himself in near permanent financial need, a pattern that was to determine much of the political history of later medieval England. In the immediate term, the Angevin kings bloated themselves on arbitrary fines and exactions. Every landlord in England ultimately held his estate from the king, and the king's 'will and want' had long determined relations with his subjects. Richard, and subsequently John, not only continued the policy of their father in imposing swingeing fines on those they claimed had caused them offence, but significantly increased the pressure by speeding the terms for repayment.

To take a handful of examples, in 1193, Hervey Bagod, a Staffordshire landowner, offered 200 marks (just over £130, since one mark = two-thirds of a pound) to succeed to a major estate. In the following year, when King Richard returned from his captivity, the fine was raised to 300 marks (£200). Roger Bigod, earl of Norfolk, offered 100 marks for protection against arbitrary seizure of his lands without judgment in court: a response to the royal protection racket whereby the king could threaten to overturn even the most clear-cut of judicial decisions should the price or the circumstances be right. In 1196, however, when Roger was serving on campaign with the king in Normandy, the fine was raised from 100 to 700 marks, and Roger found himself obliged to discharge the entire debt in less than a year. This was a protection racket forced to meet extraordinary pressures, determined to squeeze the last possible ounce of silver from those who fell within its toils. Kingship itself, for the first time in 200 years, was starved of resources. The bewildered king reacted, as mob bosses are accustomed to react, with vicious and arbitrary demands that his subjects pay the shortfall.

John's treaty with the King of France paved the way for a French seizure of much of southern and eastern Normandy, so that during the last five years of his reign, King Richard was engaged in permanent warfare in France. The costs here were met through fines, through military campaigns intended to grab treasure and the spoils of war, and through increased demands for 'scutage' (a tax payable by those who held land from the king but who failed to discharge their military service in person). The unprecedented levels of 'scutage' demanded by Richard led to a political crisis in the late 1190s, when the English bishops sought, unsuccessfully, to evade all payments charged for campaigns conducted outside the realm of England. The king's craving for treasure led directly to Richard's own death in 1199, since it was whilst campaigning in southern France, laying siege to a castle where treasure was reported to be hidden, that Richard was struck by a crossbow bolt and died, after a few days of typically futile heroics.

John, meanwhile, had been pardoned his rebellion. When Richard returned from captivity in 1194, he chose to forgive. 'He is only a boy', Richard is said to have announced of his by now 27-year-old younger brother. Although kept out of England, John remained in a key position in Normandy, waiting in the wings whilst the childless Richard sought to rebuild their father's French estate. At his death, Richard left two possible successors: John, and Arthur of Brittany – John and Richard's nephew, born in 1187 shortly after the death of his father, John's elder brother, Geoffrey, duke of Brittany. A 12-year-old boy in 1199, Arthur was in no real position to challenge John, even though there were some who favoured his claims, and even though English law supplied no clear guidance as to whether inheritance should pass to the son of an elder brother (Arthur) or to a younger sibling (John).

In 1199, there were nonetheless already signs that John would prove neither a kind uncle nor an ideal king. According to a story reported in the *Life of St Hugh of Lincoln*, John visited the site of Richard's burial at the great abbey of Fontevraud on the Loire. There he was conducted on a tour of the abbey by the saintly bishop of Lincoln. He was shown the images to the left of the entrance portal of the abbey church of evil kings burning in hell, clearly with the intention that he put aside evil and embrace the good. John, however, pointed to the images of good kings ascending into heaven on the other side of the portal, before boasting of a jewel hung around his neck, by whose power he claimed he was guaranteed never to lose his lands in France. At Mass, he hesitated over whether to give the traditional royal offering of coin: a sign of his impiety revealed once again, a year later, when during St Hugh's Easter Mass, John sent a note up to the bishop not one but three times, begging Hugh to cut short his sermon so that the king might dine.

In a treaty negotiated in May 1200, John bargained away parts of southern Normandy to the king of France in the hope that this would buy permanent peace. At almost exactly the same time, however, he embarked on a course of action that, within three years, was to doom his 'empire' to destruction. In August 1200, he married Isabella, heiress to the southern French county of Angoulême. There was sense to this union, since the neighbouring counties of Angoulême, Limoges, and Périgueux had long threatened to disrupt communications between Plantagenet Gascony and the king's lands north of the Loire. It was in imposing his authority within this region that Richard had met his death in 1199. Nonetheless, there were objections to John's marriage that affected both bride and groom. To marry Isabella, John had to divorce his first wife, Isabella of Gloucester, to whom he had been betrothed since the late 1180s. In the aftermath, he not only held on to the Gloucester estates, including the town of Bristol, but effectively consigned his former wife to house arrest, often in the vicinity or even in the same lodgings as his new French bride. The impediments to the marriage of Isabella of Angoulême were even greater. She was already betrothed to the neighbouring French baron, Hugh de Lusignan, lord of La Marche. Yet Hugh had held back from consummating the marriage, almost certainly because Isabella was considered under age. An English chronicler claims that, on her arrival in England in 1200, she appeared to be about 12 years old. In reality, she could have been as young as 8.

By making off with his child bride, John provoked Hugh de Lusignan and the barons of Poitou into rebellion. Joined with Arthur of Brittany, the rebels attempted to besiege the king's mother, Eleanor of Aquitaine, in the castle of Mirebeau north of Poitiers. Their attack brought about the one great military triumph in John's career. With lightning speed, John surprised the rebels and took the majority of them prisoner. Triumph, however, rapidly dissolved into disaster when the most significant of these prisoners, Arthur of Brittany, disappeared. Precisely what happened remains unknown. Some alleged that Arthur was murdered at the command of the king. Some claimed that he had fallen from the tower of the castle of Rouen, attempting to escape. Whatever his precise fate, Arthur and his disappearance forged a great alliance against King John. Summoned to the court of King Philip of France to explain Arthur's fate, John refused to attend. Philip declared John's continental lands to be forfeit.

Through careful management, the king of France was now almost certainly richer in cash resources than the king of England. Not only were John's lands in Normandy unable to bear the costs of near continuous defensive warfare, but the Norman aristocracy had grown to resent the transformation of their lands into a battle zone. By the 1190s, the vast majority of Anglo-Norman landowning families had divided into branches holding estates in either England or Normandy. Save for the king and a handful of the wealthiest magnates, there were precious few truly Anglo-Norman families left to defend the Anglo-Norman settlement. John himself, as count of Mortain before 1199, had chiefly encouraged those with lands in England at his court, neglecting or being cold-shouldered by his specifically Norman subjects.

As a result, within less than two years of Arthur's disappearance in 1202, a French army swept John and his supporters from Normandy and all their French territories as far south as the banks of the Loire. Even the Plantagenet family mausoleum at Fontevraud, where Henry II and Richard lay buried, henceforth stood in territory ruled by the kings of France. Only the southernmost parts of Poitou, and Gascony with its capital at Bordeaux, remained under Plantagenet control. The date generally accepted for this 'Loss of Normandy' is 1204, the year in which the ducal capital, Rouen, fell to the French.

No king could suffer military defeat on this scale without it being interpreted as proof of the withdrawal of God's favour. Moreover, since John was henceforth committed to the reconquest of his continental empire yet confined to his lands in England, the king's demand for cash for reconquest was now added to the already extensive burden of grievances against royal profligacy and extortion built up during the reign of Richard. The king himself, previously a distant figure, often absent in France, was now established permanently on the doorsteps of his English barons whose silver he coveted and against whose wives and daughters he was now rumoured to cast lascivious glances. The events of the past few years had branded John a failure for his loss of Normandy, as a lecher for his second marriage, and as a murderer for his disposal of his nephew, Arthur. His reputation was irreparably destroyed.

Something of the spirit of John's court can be recaptured from his government records as they survive from 1199 onwards. Indeed, the emergence of these royal records – enrolled copies after 1199 of the majority of the king's outgoing letters – has in itself been interpreted as evidence both of John's suspicious nature and of his pressing demand for cash. Only those who have to calculate profit and loss on a near daily basis are inclined to keep records on the scale maintained by King John's Exchequer and Chancery. From these records, in the immediate aftermath of the capture of Arthur, we read of the king devising passwords for those seeking access to his prisoners, and of John's tendency to forget the passwords that he himself had invented. Many reveal a seamier side to court life: the king's taking of the sons and nephews of his barons as hostages for future good behaviour, his payment of a bounty for the scalps of Welsh outlaws, his gifts of flowers and favours to his mistresses. Richard Marsh, later royal chancellor and bishop of Durham, commemorated for his love of beer rather than religion, extracted 'blank' charters from monasteries, sealed with their seals obliging them to abide by whatever terms the king or his agents might care to write onto the parchment. Hugh de Neville, the king's chief forester, adopted a similar practice towards state prisoners, obliging them to seal charters agreeing to the direst of penalties should they attempt to escape, yet himself supplying these men with seals so that they had no choice but to sign. In 1210, the Pipe Roll records that the major northern baron 'Robert de Vaux owes five of the best horses so that the King should shut his mouth about the wife of Henry Pinel'. Whatever the scandal here, this was a world of less than comfortable domesticity. We also have a notorious fine, recorded in 1200, whereby 'The wife of Hugh de Neville offers the King 200 chickens so that she may lie one night with her husband'. Was Hugh's wife, as some historians have proposed, attempting to escape from service as the king's mistress in order briefly to rejoin her husband, or was this a joking reference to the fact that Hugh's duties deprived his wife of company? In either case, the fact that Hugh, his wife, and both of the king's betrothed (his former wife, Isabella of Gloucester, and his present queen, Isabella of Angoulême) were lodged for long periods at Hugh's castle at Marlborough must have led to some very peculiar encounters. The fact that Hugh, although a trusted royal official, was one of those royalists who, after 1215, threw in his lot with the rebel barons, opening the gates of Marlborough to the king's enemies, suggests that, in his case, as in many others, the ties of loyalty between the king and even his closest henchman threatened to fray or snap.

One of the consequences of the king's loss of his continental estates had been to drive into exile many dozens of Frenchmen, lacking any previous connection or landed estate in England. Compromised by their service to the Plantagenets before 1204, such men were so useful to the king that they were offered sanctuary across the Channel. One such man, Peter de Maulay, it was rumoured, had actually carried out the murder of Arthur at John's command. Peter was nonetheless promoted to rich estates in England including custody of Corfe Castle in Dorset and marriage to a northern heiress by whom he came into possession of the honours of Doncaster and Mulgrave in Yorkshire. John's favour, however, was a fickle commodity. In 1212, Peter de Maulay was himself the victim of a series of guarantees extracted from his fellow courtiers, including provisions that the son of the earl of Cornwall be whipped and the earl of Salisbury give the king all his hawks should Peter cause offence: almost certainly another of John's cruel jokes. This was a court consumed by angst and racked with paranoia. As such, it stands in rather surprising contrast to the court of Henry II, John's father, where for all of the complaints about the inconstancy of fortune, and despite the murder of one particularly unfortunate former courtier, Thomas Becket, those promoted as the king's friends tended to keep not only their places but their profits.

John's French friends, led by the French-born bishop of Winchester, Peter des Roches, played a murky role at court. Des Roches, one of the richest bishops in Europe, promoted to Winchester in the immediate aftermath of the loss of Normandy, became involved in all manner of business from negotiations with other European rulers to the presentation of love tokens to the king's lady friends. Another such Frenchman, Girard d'Athée, with his sons and nephews from much the same region around Tours from which Des Roches had sprung, controlled many of the more significant of the king's castles in the English south-west: Bristol, Gloucester, Hereford. So unpopular were Girard and his kinsmen that Hugh of Wells, once a king's friend, subsequently elected bishop of Lincoln, was prepared to offer 40 marks to a Nottinghamshire knight in order to save his son from marrying Girard's daughter.

Girard d'Athée played a leading role, together with another foreigner, Fawkes de Bréauté, a Norman adventurer, in the administration of south Wales. Their interventions here were the consequence of the king's attacks upon yet another disgraced courtier, William de Braose, who in 1208 had been dramatically stripped of his lands and favours and forced into exile, first in Ireland then in France. Quite what inspired this disgrace remains uncertain, but one possibility is that William de Braose or his wife had spoken rather too openly of the circumstances in which the king's nephew, Arthur, met his death. Braose's wife and eldest son, it was alleged, were then starved to death by King John, locked up in either Windsor or Corfe Castle. The king's attack upon the Braose estates in Wales was undertaken, so the king himself proclaimed, according to the 'law of the Exchequer': in other words, as the result of William's failure to meet the terms of his financial obligations to the king, not governed by equity or customary English law. Even so, the fact that the king considered it necessary to compose and preserve a long written justification of his actions against William, and even to claim that William's subsequent outlawry, the result of his inability to pay a crushing fine of 50,000 marks, was enforced 'according to the law and custom of England', suggests an anxiety on the king's behalf to be seen to act justly however unjust such actions were in practice.

Meanwhile, the presence of so many foreigners so close to the king began to inspire native English outcry against the king's Frenchmen, now denigrated as 'aliens', enemies of the English people and of English liberties. Precisely those accusations which John himself had first raised against the regime of his brother in the 1190s were now brought to bear against John and his inner circle of henchmen, described by the chronicler Roger of Wendover as John's 'evil counsellors'. Wendover's list is of particular interest since it suggests a court dominated by a very small circle of royalist barons and placemen, only a few of them Normans or 'aliens' from south of the Loire, most of them in fact Anglo-Norman barons from families long settled in England, very close in age to the king, born in the 1160s or 1170s. This stands in marked contrast to the courts of John's father and elder brother where there had been a much more diverse mingling of generations, and where the earls and bishops had tended to play a more prominent role. It is also noticeable that several of John's closest henchmen died in the years around 1210, perhaps depriving the king of counsel that might otherwise have carried him safely through the final years of his reign.

This was a world of rumour and intrigue. In 1212, for example, it was falsely reported that the queen, Isabella of Angoulême, had been raped at Marlborough and her youngest son slain together with his tutors. Two years later, when the king returned from a disastrous expedition to France, he sent the following letter to his henchman Theodoric the German ('Terry the Teuton'):

> Know that we are well and unharmed, and...we shall shortly be coming to your parts, and we shall be thinking of you like a hawk. And although we may have been absent for ten years, when we come to you it shall seem to us as if we had been away no more than three days. Take care of the thing entrusted to you, letting us know frequently how it fares.

This is a letter that only makes sense when we realize that Theodoric had recently been appointed chief guardian of the queen. The 'thing' entrusted to him was Isabella of Angoulême, so that the letter should be read either as a covert message of love directed by John to his absent wife, or more realistically, as a threat that the queen and her guardian were being closely watched.

To John's catalogue of crimes, after 1205 was added a final self-inflicted injury: an open breach with the Church. Since the murder of Thomas Becket in 1170, although obliged to tread warily, the kings of England had been allowed very much their own way in appointments to bishoprics. In 1205, for example, and despite some resistance, John had been able to secure Winchester for his henchman Peter des Roches. Determined to prevent another such infringement of ecclesiastical privilege, in the following year the pope, Innocent III, refused all inducements to promote a courtier as successor to the late archbishop of Canterbury, Hubert Walter. Instead, in a process almost as murky as the royal intrigues against which it was directed, the pope secured promotion to Canterbury for a scholar in late middle age, a master at the schools of Paris and quite possibly the pope's own former tutor, Master Stephen Langton. Sprung from a family of minor Lincolnshire knights, Langton was in many ways a peculiar choice, famed more for his work as a commentator on the Bible than for any political or administrative expertise. For at least the past twenty years, he had taught in Paris, a fact that in itself would have disqualified him in the eyes of King John, since Paris was the home of John's arch-enemy, Philip Augustus, recently the conqueror of Normandy.

Langton's Bible commentaries can appear dry as dust: thousands of pages of explanation of the meanings of scriptural words or phrases, the vast majority of them still unpublished, as indigestible today as to the students who, 800 years ago, laboured to make sense of them. Yet amidst this vast torrent of words are secreted nuggets of pure political gold. The Old Testament, after all, tells the story of good and bad kings and their attempts to enforce or evade God's laws. Langton was not slow to draw modern parallels. The kings of Scripture, he argued, had been wise to arm themselves with a *Deuteronomy*, a book of laws, set down with the aid of the priesthood. By contrast, modern rulers sought to evade both the advice of their priests and the obligation to rule according to written law. 'Necessity', or absolute need, Langton argued, was the sole justification for taxation as set out in the Bible, yet modern rulers taxed for trivial reasons, from mere vanity or pride. Those who attended Langton's lectures would have heard him contrast the priesthood recruited by Moses with modern bishops 'recruited from the Exchequer in London'. Those who read his commentary on the book of *Chronicles* would have found him railing 'against princes who flee from lengthy sermons', surely a reference to King John's attempts to escape the sermonizing of St Hugh of Lincoln. Kingship itself, Langton argued, had been decreed by God not as reward but as a punishment to mankind. As the Old Testament book of *Hosea* (13:11) proclaims, 'I have given you a king in my wrath'.

Historians in search of an 'author' for Magna Carta have on occasion advanced the claims of Stephen Langton, even though there is little evidence to suggest that it was he in person who drafted the document. Far more significant was the impact of Langton's exile from England after 1208, leading in 1209 to the imposition of a sentence of papal 'interdict'. For the next five years, the laity were in theory excluded from the sacraments of the Church: no Mass, no burial in consecrated ground. The king was threatened with personal excommunication. The majority of England's bishops fled into exile. From this, a number of consequences flowed. The public display of the king's impiety compounded the sense that John had flouted God's laws. Some claimed that the king was considering conversion to Islam, or that the pope had licensed John's deposition, empowering a French army to cross the Channel and seize the English throne in defence of Christendom and with the same privileges as a crusade. Neither rumour was true. Nonetheless, with a French fleet massing on the Flemish coast, and with the threat of rebellion from both the Welsh and the Irish, in 1212 John was forced into a sudden change of policy. On 1 June, still oblivious to the gathering storm, he ordered an inquest into knights' fees and the rights of the crown on a scale that, had it been completed, might have rivalled the Domesday survey of 1086. Simultaneously, a judicial visitation or 'eyre' of the northern forests of England imposed fines and punishments unprecedented even for a notoriously rapacious administration. By mid-August, made aware of the threats against him, the king had abandoned both his great inquest and his forest enquiry.

Rumours began to circulate not just of rebellion but of something far more serious: a baronial plot either to kill the king or to lure him into death in battle against the Welsh. John was forced to call off his Welsh campaign and to deal with the alleged conspirators. To this end, in August 1212, he summoned six knights from every county of England to attend his court. This summons (itself significant as the first precedent for the summoning of knights of the shires to take counsel with the king, later a key element in the constitution of the English Parliament) led to the suggestion that two particular barons, Robert fitz Walter and Eustace de Vescy, were responsible for plotting the king's death. Both men had cause for discontent. Rumours that the king planned to seduce Robert's daughter and Eustace's wife were almost certainly false. Nonetheless, both men were major landholders, Eustace in Northumberland, Robert chiefly in Essex. Both had been involved in John's unsuccessful wars in Normandy and had lost lands as a result. Both were closely related to a network of English barons most of whom by now smarted under financial grievances exacerbated by more than fifty years of Plantagenet rule. Both now fled into exile, Eustace to Scotland, Robert to France.

There are similarities between the events of 1212 and the last great baronial rebellion against a Plantagenet king, in 1173–4. Both in 1173 and in 1212, baronial rebellion seems to have followed contingently from attempts by the king to survey the landholding and financial resources of his barons. Intriguingly, both in 1173 and in 1212, rebellion followed soon after royal expeditions to Ireland, by Henry II in 1171–2 and by John in 1210: expeditions that perhaps offered rather too practical a demonstration of the ways in which an angry king might rule if left to his own arbitrary devices. Nearly 200 years later, similar things were to happen as a result of King Richard II's Irish expedition of 1399. There was nonetheless one key distinction between the rebellion of 1173–4 and that which began to gather pace in England after 1212. The rebels of the 1170s, led by Henry's own son, failed in their attempts to make common cause with the Church, despite their claims to be acting in the name of the recently martyred St Thomas of Canterbury. After 1212, there is evidence that the rebels against

King John, led by barons rather than by any malcontent Plantagenet prince, were able to call upon a far more active alliance with ecclesiastical opinion.

The fact that, throughout this period, the archbishop of Canterbury, Stephen Langton, was exiled in France, served to strengthen this alliance between Church and rebels. Langton himself played up the association between his own exile and that of the martyred St Thomas Becket, using a seal that showed Becket's martyrdom as a symbol of Langton's own resistance to royal tyranny. These same years witnessed a more general sense of crisis throughout Christendom provoked by events in southern France. There, since 1208, a crusade had been in progress against a sect dubbed the 'Cathars' or 'Albigensians': heretics who rejected the authority of the pope and whose extirpation had provided an opportunity for the barons of northern France to seize the rich southern lands of the Languedoc. The fact that King John appeared to support the heretics, maintaining communications with his cousins, the counts of Toulouse, and even supporting an anti-French alliance between Toulouse and the kings of northern Spain, only increased the sense that John himself was an agent of anti-Christ. In July 1212, at more or less precisely the same time that the baronial conspiracy emerged at his court, a great fire engulfed London Bridge. This too was interpreted by contemporaries in an apocalyptic sense, as proof that London itself had suffered the fate of Old Testament Sodom. In the north of England, John was the subject of prophecies broadcast by a hermit, Peter of Wakefield, claiming that the king would lose his crown by the forthcoming feast of the Ascension (23 May 1213). Amongst the rumours circulating by now was one that the rebel barons had already selected a candidate to replace King John. Their choice is said to have fallen on the ultra-orthodox Simon de Montfort, leader of the Albigensian crusade: yet further proof of the degree to which King John was reckoned to have forfeited God's favour.

All of this helps to explain the king's decision not only to call off his inquests into land and forests but to make peace with the Church. The settlement negotiated with the pope in the spring of 1213 was timed for the eve of Ascension Day, thereby disproving the prophecies of Peter of Wakefield who was himself put to death, torn apart between galloping horses as his body was brought for execution. By the end of May 1213, news had reached England of the destruction of the French fleet gathered off the Flemish coast. Nonetheless, John's settlement with the Church did little to silence rumour. For a start, it resulted in no immediate lifting of the Interdict, delayed for more than a year until terms had been agreed for compensation to be paid to the Church and the exiled bishops. This was accompanied by a deliberate linking of the grievances of clergy and barons, so that the cause of the exiled conspirators, Robert fitz Walter and Eustace de Vescy, was now taken up by the Church with demands that they be restored to the king's peace. This was of great significance. It confirmed that the exiled clergy, led by Stephen Langton, not only sought to appeal to the needs of a community of all the faithful, the 'communitas fidelium', but that, for the first time since Becket and the great rebellion of the 1170s, dissident clergy and barons were brought together into a godly alliance directed against an ungodly English king. Furthermore, the settlement of May 1213, far from refuting the prophecies of Peter of Wakefield, seemed in some minds proof that Peter's claims had come true. In a device intended to ensure the pope's protection against his enemies in France, John now declared England and Ireland to be papal fiefdoms.

At Dover in May 1213, perhaps laying his crown before him on the ground, John knelt before the pope's representatives and offered a perpetual annual tribute of 1,000 marks. There were precedents here. The kingdom of Sicily had long been regarded as a papal fief. Portugal had been claimed as such since the 1170s, and in 1204, the King of Aragon had placed his lands under the protection of Innocent III, once again as a feudal vassal. Aragon was in particularly close negotiation with King John throughout the years of the papal Interdict, as John's chief ally with Toulouse against the French. None of this, however, served to lessen the sense of shock that John's actions induced. To contemporaries, particularly to monastic chroniclers fiercely protective of the independence of their own oligarchic institutions, this appeared nothing short of abject surrender on the king's behalf. Having lost Normandy and his continental lands to the French, John was now prepared to subject his own realm of England to papal authority.

Chapter 4
The road to Runnymede

Much of the outrage against John's dealings with the pope was expressed only in hindsight, years later, when John's manoeuvres had long been exposed as failures. At the time, John had cause to hope for better things. With the pope now an ally, and with the threat of a French invasion averted, John could employ the vast treasure that he had built up over the previous ten years, to launch precisely that campaign of reconquest in France of which he had long dreamed. The wealth of England and of the English Church, tapped mercilessly since 1204, now lay at the king's disposal. An attempt in the spring of 1213 to carry war to the French nonetheless ended in fiasco, when a series of summonses to his barons met with widespread resistance. Reviving the complaint first voiced by the bishops of the 1190s, that their service should be limited to England alone, a significant number of barons refused to join the king's army summoned to sail for Poitou.

There were two consequences here. The first was that John was unable to send an army to France. In September 1213, and without English support, his chief allies in the south, the King of Aragon and the Count of Toulouse, suffered a crushing defeat by the French. At the battle of Muret outside Toulouse, John's southern alliance crumbled to dust. Secondly, the resistance of the English barons led to a widespread perception that there now existed a significant constituency of baronial opposition to the king.

Contemporaries, from 1213 onwards, began to refer to this group of malcontents as the 'Northerners'. In so far as they can be identified, the barons in question held their lands not only in Northumberland and Cumbria but in Yorkshire, Lincolnshire, and the north Midlands: a region that had suffered particularly exploitative government for the past ten years. It was to buy off this opposition that, in the final months of 1213, John sought terms. After a three-week tour of the north, accompanied by the full panoply of his hounds and his hawks, clearly intended to show off the sheer brute power at his disposal, on 1 November 1213, the king met with the 'Northerners' at Wallingford. There, through the mediation of the Church, he seems to have made some sort of promise to uphold ancient liberties. A week later, nonetheless, he commanded all knights summoned to a council at Oxford to come armed, whilst the barons were to appear in person and unarmed. This was a blatant attempt to intimidate the barons, and as such typical of John's combination of unreliability and guile. This was a king whose promises could never be trusted.

In the short term, threats proved effective where promises failed. In the winter of 1213, John began disbursing his vast store of treasure, to buy allies in France, to purchase the support of the claimant to the Holy Roman Empire, the Saxon ruler Otto IV, and to win over the barons of Flanders to his cause. Two great armies were to be launched from England. The first, commanded by the king's half-brother, William 'Longsword', earl of Salisbury, would join with the Germans and Flemings to attack France from the north. John himself would cross to Poitou and thence attack from south of the Loire. This was truly a grand alliance, financed by a war chest raised from taxation and other profits of government equivalent to the treasure expended in the Norman Conquest of 1066, or indeed, in comparative terms, in the D-Day landings of 1944. Yet even before its launch, there were signs that not all would go according to plan.

To begin with, the alliance with Toulouse and Aragon upon which John had pinned his hopes for the past few years had now disintegrated, with the King of Aragon slain on the battlefield of Muret and the Count of Toulouse, long a suspected heretic, forced into exile in England. William 'Longsword', appointed by John as commander of his northern alliance, was a peculiar choice as king's friend. The illegitimate son of John's father, Henry II, born to one of Henry II's many mistresses, William's background supplied startling evidence of Plantagenet family disfunctionality. If modern research is to be trusted, William's mother, subsequently countess of Norfolk, was herself the cousin of one woman and the daughter of another both of whom had previously shared Henry II's bed. It is surely indicative of King John's wider failure that, whereas his father had managed to commit adultery on an heroic scale and even to live down the murder of St Thomas Becket, John's own crimes, both of violence and of lust, were met with fury and ultimately with retribution. Henry II was a successful tyrant; John was not. Finally, the king's chosen governor for England during his absence, Peter des Roches, bishop of Winchester, was leader of that 'alien' faction at court most distrusted by the English barons. Des Roches's appointment was provocative both to the barons and to the Church, led by Stephen Langton, whose exile Des Roches had refused to join and against whose claims for financial compensation and 'free' elections to English bishoprics and monasteries he continued to work.

In England itself, there were further tensions, personal as well as political. In January 1214, John negotiated one of his more notorious pieces of financial business, auctioning off his first wife, Isabella of Gloucester, to Geoffrey de Mandeville, earl of Essex, for a vast fine of 20,000 marks. The terms of this fine were such that Geoffrey had no real prospect of paying. Moreover, since Isabella had been married to John for ten years in the 1190s without producing offspring and was by now almost certainly beyond child-bearing age, Geoffrey could hope for few long-term gains from such a marriage. The fine, and Geoffrey's subsequent struggles with the Exchequer, were merely the most dramatic of the many dozens of such disputes that had punctuated John's reign. The effect was to throw Geoffrey, now earl of both Essex and Gloucester, into the camp of the malcontents, significantly tipping the balance of power from king to barons.

All might still have gone well. William 'Longsword' enjoyed considerable military success in Flanders. In Poitou, John made contact with the local aristocracy in the expectation of future gains. On Sunday 27 July 1214, however, there came a mighty fall at the battle of Bouvines, fought a few miles to the south-east of Lille. Against the advice of William 'Longsword', the northern army's knights charged the French and were slaughtered or captured in the aftermath. John himself was several hundred miles away, but the defeat of his northern alliance spelled an end to all his gains in the south. A decisive turning point in the history of France, guaranteeing that Philip Augustus would retain his territorial conquests of the past twenty years, Bouvines was a disaster for King John, its consequences in many ways as significant as those of the Battle of Hastings fought 150 years earlier. The road from Bouvines to Magna Carta was both straight and speedy. It is nonetheless some indication of his alleged inability to comprehend the full extent of the disaster that, in the aftermath of Bouvines, with William 'Longsword' held captive by the French, King John is said to have attempted the seduction of William's wife. Old habits, like old rumours, die hard.

Already, by the time the battle was fought, a number of the English barons had signalled their disapproval of the king, refusing either to serve in person in John's continental armies or to pay the 'scutage' demanded from those who stayed at home. In effect, this represented a tax strike: the first signal of the coming storm. It gathered pace after Bouvines, with several barons, including the earls of Winchester and Norfolk who had sent service to Poitou, now defecting to the malcontents. John returned from Poitou in October 1214, his treasure gone, the extraordinary efforts of the past ten years thrown away in a single day's combat. Attempts were made to buy off the opposition. The king granted a charter of 'free' elections to the Church, modelled upon offers made by Henry I in his coronation charter of 1100, and by the King of Aragon in the face of baronial opposition as recently as 1207. Although the Interdict was lifted in November 1214, before full compensation had been paid to the English bishops, the king himself took the extraordinary step, on Ash Wednesday, 4 March 1215, of declaring himself a Crusader, pledged to embark with a Crusading army to the East. A few token gestures were made towards fulfilling this vow. A ship was prepared, but almost certainly as a potential escape capsule rather than as a real bid to fight in the Holy Land. The true purpose of John's vows was to place himself and his realm more deeply under papal protection. As a Crusader he sought to make himself immune from attack at the hands of fellow Christians, including by now not only the king of France but John's own barons.

The emergence of baronial opposition remains a murky and a poorly documented affair. We have a number of claims by the chroniclers, and a small selection of documents, all of which point to 1214 and the aftermath of Bouvines as the turning point in affairs. Nonetheless, even before the king embarked for France, rebellion was in the air. The coalition of interests between the English bishops and the leaders of the failed revolt of 1212, Robert fitz Walter and Eustace de Vescy, and the subsequent emergence of the 'Northerners' and their claims mediated by the Church in the autumn of 1213, were highly significant. In 1215, Robert fitz Walter was to style himself 'Marshal of the Army of God' in his role as rebel commander, perhaps parodying the title 'marshal' applied by the king to those supposedly mustering the king's forces for Crusade: a potent reminder of the degree to which the rebels now saw themselves as champions of a holy cause.

According to the chronicler Roger of Wendover, perhaps as early as August 1213, Archbishop Stephen Langton had drawn public attention to Henry I's coronation charter as a potential model for baronial dealings with John. The chronology and the factual accuracy of the chroniclers' account of these events have both been challenged. Wendover alleges that, perhaps in July 1213 and as part of John's settlement with the Church, the king had sworn an oath to uphold the laws of Edward the Confessor: an interesting example of the way in which the (largely mythical) laws of Good King Edward remained a gold standard against which to judge later sovereigns. In all likelihood, Wendover exaggerates here. If an undertaking was made, then it probably involved nothing more than a renewal of John's coronation oaths: a promise to govern well with no specific reference to King Edward or earlier English law. Again, according to Wendover, probably in July 1213, the archbishop and various barons met with the king's ministers at Roger's own monastery of St Albans. There they were promised that the laws of Henry I would be maintained and all evil customs abolished. In the autumn of 1214, Wendover claims that the barons gathered at Bury St Edmunds and swore a collective oath to make war on the king should he fail to confirm Henry I's coronation charter. Neither of these meetings is otherwise documented. Both may be fictitious, though this has done nothing to discourage the modern municipal authorities of Bury St Edmunds and St Albans from claiming status as 'Magna Carta towns', intimately associated with the charter's negotiation.

Roger of Wendover was writing a decade later and with a particular interest in exaggerating the degree to which his own and other monasteries had mustered opposition to the king. In reality, our first certain proof that Henry I's coronation charter was being cited in negotiations between king and barons occurs only at a later stage, with the survival of the so-called 'Unknown Charter', a document rediscovered in the French national archives in the 1890s, today one of the best-known 'unknown' documents in English history. It consists of a single sheet of parchment on which are written first a copy of Henry I's coronation charter, undertaking to rule well, and second a series of a dozen or so clauses beginning with the statement 'King John conceeds that he will arrest no man without judgement nor accept any payment for justice nor commit any unjust act': in embryo, our first evidence for what was to evolve into the famous clauses 39 and 40 of Magna Carta. The exact date of the 'Unknown Charter' is disputed. It most likely records bargaining points raised between king and barons at some stage in 1215. Various of its clauses may already have been under discussion for some time before. For example, its attempt to limit military service overseas to Normandy and Brittany and to limit scutage to one mark per knight's fee, not subsequently embodied in Magna Carta, seem to refer to the situation of 1213–14 when service was demanded for Flanders and Poitou and when multiple scutages were collected.

Here, as elsewhere, the 'Unknown Charter' is more adventurous than Magna Carta. In respect to wards and widows and to the need to 'disafforest' all land placed under forest law since 1154, it goes beyond anything subsequently granted in Magna Carta. What is most significant of all is that it treats the new concessions offered by King John quite literally as extensions of privileges already guaranteed by the coronation charter of Henry I, itself claiming merely to restore the good law of Edward the Confessor. In other words, the barons of 1215 believed that good law had once existed and that their duty lay in recalling and restoring it. To this extent, Magna Carta is to be viewed as a deeply conservative, not as a deliberately radical, measure.

Its negotiation was the result of a series of meetings between king and barons, beginning in January 1215, when a council in London merely postponed any further discussion to the following April. Having delayed this April meeting for as long as possible, the king offered to seek arbitration from the pope. From a baronial standpoint, this was no real offer, since the pope would be naturally predisposed to support the king. John, after all, had surrendered the realm of England to papal sovereignty. Moreover, no pope could accept a settlement extracted from a reluctant king, God's anointed, under threat of violence and rebellion. It was a principle deeply embedded in canon as in civil law that a settlement obtained under duress was no true contract. Instead, when the barons gathered at Brackley in May 1215, they opened hostilities by repudiating their homage to King John. Their choice of Brackley as meeting place is significant. Brackley served as one of the chief tournament fields of England, and it was perhaps on the tournament field that the barons had first begun to whisper the need to impose restrictions upon the king. On 12 May, the king ordered the seizure of the barons' castles. Five days later, fate once more dealt John a crushing blow. Whilst its leading citizens were at Mass, a small group of Londoners, in league with the barons, seized John's capital and effectively deprived the king of both the chief citadel and treasure house of his realm. Henceforth, the demands of the Londoners were joined to those of the barons. There was now a real prospect that London would serve as a base from which to organize the most disastrous of possibilities: an invitation to the French king to replace the Plantagenet dynasty on the throne of England.

The Londoners had grievances of their own against the king. Their trade had been disrupted by John's recent wars in Flanders and Poitou. From at least the 1150s, the more adventurous of them had demanded the right to self-government. Indeed, the self-government and chartered privileges of the greater English towns served as yet another model for the sort of chartered liberties that Magna Carta was intended to supply. And not just the towns of England. On Easter Sunday, 19 April 1215, in the midst of the gathering storm, King John issued a charter to the men of the town of Bayonne, on the frontiers between France and Spain, now granted the same privileges as the men of La Rochelle, another of the major southern French ports still in Plantagenet hands. This in effect gave recognition to the government of Bayonne by a commune and council of 100, yet another of those detailed provisions for communal self-government that deserve to be seen as steps on the road to Magna Carta.

As this should remind us, Magna Carta could boast continental as well as English precedents. Many of these emerged from precisely those parts of Spain and southern France where King John had been diplomatically most active in the years before 1215. In 1205, for example, in the midst of a financial crisis provoked by the costs of war, King Pedro II of Aragon drafted but apparently did not grant a charter of liberties for his subjects in Catalonia, promising an end to new or excessive taxes, the appointment of local men as royal officials to administer 'common justice' and to preserve the right and custom of the land, such officials only to be appointed 'with the counsel of magnates and the wise men of that land'. North of the Pyrenees but still within the same jurisprudential orbit, in December 1212, Simon de Montfort, leader of the Albigensian Crusade, had issued the so-called 'Statute of Pamiers', the only one of these southern constitutional documents that approaches the scale of the 1215 English Magna Carta, amongst other things forbidding the sale of justice, legislating on the disposition of heirs, marriage portions, and the remarriage of widows, and specifying that the rulers of the new Crusading state of Toulouse and Narbonne were not entitled to service save by grace and at the ruler's pay. Ten of the eleven opening clauses of the Statute of Pamiers guaranteed the maintenance of ecclesiastical liberties and discipline.

The Statute of Pamiers supplied precedents for King John's Magna Carta, which deals with just such feudal 'incidents' and which itself opens with an undertaking, granted to God, that 'The English Church be free'. Statutes issued by a papal legate at Bordeaux in 1214, carefully copied into King John's chancery rolls, state that widows should not be compelled by princes to remarry, a provision directly echoed in Magna Carta, clause 8. In proclaiming the outlawry of Robert fitz Walter and his fellow conspirators, processed via the county court of Essex in 1212–13, the king had been assiduous in respecting the particular customs of the shire, itself a concept dear to the authors of Magna Carta with their demand that respect be shown to customary law (clauses 2, 4, 13, 23, 41, 48, 60). The 'customs of England' are again referred to in royal letters as early as 1204, proclaiming as a matter of principle that no under-age ward be summoned to give evidence as to landholding, such pleas being delayed until the ward came of age: principles very close to those enshrined in Magna Carta, clauses 4–5.

This is not to suggest that Magna Carta was simply the adaptation to the particular circumstances of 1215 of legislation already existing in England, France, or Spain. On the contrary, the negotiation of Magna Carta was a complicated business, hammered out between king and barons over the course of weeks or months. These negotiations themselves suggest a sophisticated knowledge of the law and of legal terminology now shared between king and barons, the inevitable consequence of the great leap forwards in English legal practice from the 1170s onwards. To this extent, the search for a single author of Magna Carta is a futile one. There were many people in 1215, both on the royalist and the baronial side, who possessed the requisite legal literacy to dictate its clauses. The 'Unknown Charter', for example, although far from an 'official' production of the king's writing office, is already written with the same technical terminology employed in the royal law courts. Not just the coronation charter of Henry I, but the charters of towns and cities, the laws dispensed by the barons in their own manorial or honour courts, the precedents set by legislation in other parts of Europe, the laws of the Church, and the traditions of diplomacy and diplomatic negotiation, all played a part in Magna Carta's evolution. The appearance in Magna Carta of occasional items of vocabulary derived from Roman imperial law (one such is the Latin *delictum* for the word translated into English as 'offence' in Magna Carta, clause 20) is not necessarily to be read as evidence of a desire directly to copy Roman law. Most such words could be found in the Bible as well as in legal textbooks. The frontiers between Roman, Canon, and English common law were not demarcated with anything like the rigour applied in a modern university law faculty. With that magpie cunning for which they are still famed, lawyers and law-makers were prepared to borrow from whatever source of law seemed best suited to circumstance.

This was a society bred up on law, keen to derive legal precedent from whatever authority came most easily to hand. Law supplied protection, albeit flimsy and unreliable protection, against what might otherwise devolve (as in England after 1066, or during Stephen's reign of the 1140s, or in Normandy after the French conquest of 1204) into a free-for-all scramble for resources governed by little save brute force and the theoretical sovereignty of kings. Law was to society as the mind was to the body: a guiding conscience and a God-given power of reasoning by which irrational animal impulse might be tamed. From the point of view of those seeking to curb royal excess, there was only one major stumbling block. The king remained the principal mouthpiece, and in all practical effect the ultimate organizing intelligence by which law was proclaimed. Whatever God's intentions, bad kings tended to make bad laws. Whether we regard Magna Carta itself as badly or well drafted, it was a document ultimately made by and issued in the name of the very king whose excesses it was intended to curb.

None of this has prevented historians from singling out Stephen Langton, archbishop of Canterbury, as 'chief architect' of Magna Carta. We have already found Langton engaged in debates over the obligation of rulers to issue laws and, in the immediate circumstances of 1215, supposedly involved in the rediscovery of Henry I's coronation charter as a precedent for the terms now to be forced upon King John. In 1214, Langton issued a detailed set of statutes for the diocese of Canterbury, regulating the behaviour of the clergy but also including legislation targeted at the laity, forbidding the advertisement of rowdy drinking contests or the sale of justice, this last directly echoed in Magna Carta, clauses 36 and 40. Langton's statutes for Canterbury to some extent provide a 'Deuteronomy' (or guidebook) for the Christian faithful.

Nineteenth-century historians were in no doubt that Magna Carta was itself dictated by Langton. Who else but the archbishop, they argued, could have ensured that the charter, rather than protecting the essentially selfish liberties of the barons, was extended (clause 60) from the barons themselves to their own men, 'both clerk and lay'?

Langton is the first person named after the king in the opening phrases of Magna Carta, as the first of all the king's 'faithful subjects' through whose counsel the charter is said to have been granted. Clause 1 of the charter guarantees (and from this point onwards readers should refer to the text of the 1215 charter translated at the back of this volume) 'that the English Church be free', confirming the same ecclesiastical liberties acknowledged at the opening of Henry I's coronation charter, but in the circumstances of 1215 clearly invoking Langton's struggles to obtain recognition for the rights of the Church. This struggle is itself directly referred to in the confirmation (again, clause 1) of John's charter of November 1214 granting freedom of elections to the Church. All of this suggests direct input from Langton.

Yet our evidence here is by no means as clear-cut as 19th-century writers supposed. According to clause 1 of Magna Carta, the charter of free elections for the Church had first been granted of the king's free will, 'before the dispute that arose between us and our barons'. This could be read as a cunning attempt to distinguish between those things that Langton had obtained for the Church before 1215, and the circumstances in which Magna Carta itself was negotiated, by inference in the midst of open rebellion and against the king's free will. In other words, this may be a sign that far from acting as the charter's midwife, Langton sought to disassociate himself from Magna Carta save in so far as its clauses directly affected the Church. Clause 60, insisting that the liberties granted by the king to his barons be extended from the barons to their own men, far from being invented by Langton, is in effect merely a repetition of similar injunctions already to be found in Henry I's coronation charter of 1100.

One aspect of Magna Carta may still suggest Langton's specific influence. As we have seen, from 1212 onwards, the coalition between clerical and baronial opposition led to demands that the king reform his administration. The earliest precise record of these demands, set out in the 'Unknown Charter', still envisaged the king's reforms as an exercise of grace: an award of liberties, granted in the name of the king to his subjects, sealed with the king's seal, and guaranteed under royal oath. Yet Magna Carta, as issued, goes far beyond this. Although it opens as a royal charter, granted by the king, first to God (as ultimate authority), and then to 'all free men of our realm', it ends with a series of provisions that threaten to transform it from an exercise of grace into something more like a contract between king and barons. The barons, although not the king's equals, are here envisaged as a powerful constituency requiring guarantees beyond mere oaths or promises. There was sound reasoning behind this. Kings in the past had made promises, not least those set out by Henry I in his coronation charter, that they had signally failed to keep. King John was a notorious oath-breaker. Even so, the method adopted by the barons to protect Magna Carta against the king was most unusual. Besides the opening clause, granted to God (the traditional beneficiary of royal coronation charters and of charters bestowing favour upon churches or monasteries, from whom no king would dare take back concessions once made), the charter includes detailed provisions for a group of twenty-five barons who (according to clause 61, the so-called 'security' clause of the charter) 'with all their might are to observe, maintain and cause to be observed the peace and liberties (hereby) granted'.

This baronial 'committee' of twenty-five is first mentioned in negotiations in June 1215, when it is included in the so-called 'Articles of the Barons', a draft schedule of terms, very close to the final form in which Magna Carta was issued, written in an official-looking hand and sealed with the king's seal, headed 'These are the chapters which the barons seek and the King grants'. Both the 'Articles' and Magna Carta, clause 61, envisage the twenty-five barons as a deterrent force, so that if the king withdrew any of his concessions or broke any of his promises, the twenty-five might take up arms against him, seize his resources, and force him to obey the terms of the charter, using all means short of actual physical violence against him or his family. It is here that the truly radical nature of Magna Carta emerges. This was to be a peace treaty between king and barons. It was nonetheless a treaty negotiated under the extraordinary understanding that in future the barons would be permitted to make war on their king whenever they judged that the king had breached fundamental principles of the contract hereby made. It is this, above all else, that affords Magna Carta its status as the first attempt to limit the previously limitless sovereignty of kings.

Where did this idea come from, and why the number twenty-five? It has long been recognized that twenty-five, as an odd number, supplied a guarantee against split voting. Yet twenty-five is also a highly significant number in the Bible. It is, for example, the age from which God instruced Moses to permit the Levites to be consecrated to God's service (Numbers 8:24), the age at which many of the kings of Judea came to the throne (in 2 Kings and 2 Chronicles), and a number used in calculating the dimensions of the Temple according to the prophet Ezechial. In the context of Magna Carta, and much more significantly, it is also a number that occurs in the standard Latin text of the Gospel of St John (6:19), where it is reported that having witnessed Christ miraculously feeding five thousand people on only five loaves and two fishes, the disciples sailed onto the Sea of Galilee 'twenty-five or thirty furlongs' and there saw Christ walking on the waves. Commenting on this passage in his 'Tractates on John' (26:6), one of the most popular works of scriptural exegesis preserved in the libraries of medieval Europe, St Augustine had explained that the number twenty-five represents the square of five, which is a

3. The Articles of the Barons

number that itself represents the law. There are five books to the Pentateuch, the laws of Moses, just as there were five loaves feeding the five thousand. Twenty-five thus represents the 'law squared'. To anyone familiar with numerology (the medieval science of numbers), twenty-five was also the number reached by placing Christ at the head of the twelve prophets of the Old Testament combined with the twelve apostles of the New. As a result, it was a number of mystic as well as of practical significance. This may explain not only why it was chosen for the barons of Magna Carta, but again in 1258, when a council of twenty-five consisting of the king and twenty-four barons (twelve of them royalists, twelve of them against the king) was appointed to implement reforms to the government of King John's son, Henry III. It was chosen again, in the 1340s, when it was the number of knights appointed by King Edward III to his new Order of the Garter, with the king and his twenty-five knights intended to serve as models of chivalric perfection, a new Arthur and his round table dispensing Christ-like wisdom and good governance.

Was it Langton, with his biblical expertise, who first suggested the number twenty-five to the barons of King John? Perhaps not. The idea of a committee of twenty-five already occurs in 1200, when it is reported as the number of men sworn to take counsel with the mayor for the government of the city of London. It was more likely the rebel Londoners, rather than the archbishop of Canterbury, who first proposed the idea for inclusion in Magna Carta. Whoever it was proposed it, the baronial committee of twenty-five was nonetheless the measure above all others that marked a new departure from previous dealings between king and barons. This in itself reflects not just the sophistication of the political and legal negotiations that led to Magna Carta, but the much more visceral terror felt by those taking up arms against the king.

After his inconclusive discussions in January 1215, and his vows as a Crusader in March, John entered negotiations with what he assumed was very much the winning hand. Although civil war was now inevitable, it was a war, in the words of the greatest of its modern historians J. C. Holt, 'which only the King could win'. Even with twenty-five barons against him, some of them, as with Richard de Clare, earl of Hertford, claiming to command personal retinues of up to 140 knights, the king still possessed vastly superior resources, a majority of English castles now under garrison, a contingent of household knights larger than that of any baron, and the ability not only to call upon the moral assistance of the pope but to summon to his aid mercenaries from Flanders, southern France, or Ireland. Yet what is most remarkable about the drift to civil war in 1215 is its slow pace. The last great rebellion against an English king, in 1173–4, had come like a bolt out of the blue, so swiftly that no-one could explain it save as an act of divine retribution for the murder of Thomas Becket. The precedent set by the war of the 1170s was no doubt in the minds of the barons forty years later. Some indeed had been children in 1173. Although the greatest baronial uprising yet staged, the 1173 rebellion had proved a disaster for its leaders. Its outcome had been a Plantagenet administration far more ruthless than anything seen before. Baronial castles had fallen by the dozen. Earls had been imprisoned, heiresses seized. To step back into the past and once again to take up arms against the king was to risk repeating precisely the mistakes of the 1170s. Hence no doubt the decision of the conspirators of 1212 to be done with such worries and merely to kill the king. Hence the fact that, three years later, the barons of 1215 moved so slowly. King John had an evil reputation. His reign had been scarred by hostage-taking, allegations of rape, and the murder of prisoners. He seemed to operate outside the norms of chivalric behaviour. After 1204, his administration, much of it imported from France, had introduced the bitterness of twenty years of fighting in Normandy to what had previously been the warless English shires. John's misdeeds provoked baronial rebellion, but they also gave warning of the likely consequences to the rebels should rebellion fail.

At Brackley in early May, the barons threw off their homage to King John by a process known as 'diffidation', crucial in the medieval distinction between peace and war. No vassal could make war on his lord without committing treason, itself punishable by death. By publicly repudiating his vassal status, a disgruntled inferior could rebel without treason, being judged henceforth according to the customs of war. As this suggests, the potential consequences of failed rebellion still haunted the barons and inclined them towards negotiated peace. Even so, it was not until the seizure of London on 17 May, and the consequent threat that the barons would use London to summon the king of France to their aid, that John was persuaded to enter seriously into negotiations. Magna Carta, issued at Runnymede in June 1215, half way between the king's castle at Windsor and the rebel base in London, was a last attempt to restore peace. To both sides, war risked the most severe of consequences. To the king, the very survival of his dynasty seemed threatened. Unjust kings, as the Bible made only too plain, risked losing their thrones, especially if their subjects made common cause with foreign powers, with the Philistines in the case of King Saul, or the French in the case of King John. To the barons, by contrast, the chief risk was that they would be overwhelmed by the king's superior forces. In 1212, at the beginning of their troubles, various barons had plotted simply to murder John and to place their own candidate on the throne. Three years later, all they could manage was a compromise, an attempt at a peace treaty with a sovereign no longer respected but greatly feared: a king whose past promises to compromise had proved as fleeting as snow in May. Magna Carta was first and foremost a peace treaty. As a peace treaty, it entirely failed.

Chapter 5
The charter defeated: the charter victorious

Because it was intended to make peace and led only to war, Magna Carta as issued by King John in June 1215 remains a shadowy thing, of greater significance in spirit than in its practical application. Many of its clauses were still-born from the moment of issue. This was a charter issued in the name of the king, beginning with his titles (as ruler of England and Ireland and still, in his own mind, of Normandy and his Continental lands, many of them in fact lost since 1204); ending with a claim that the charter had been issued under the king's own hand 'in the meadow that is called Runnymede between Windsor and Staines, on the fifteenth day of June in the seventeenth year of our reign'. The dating clause is significant. The date of the charter, 15 June, is now generally accepted as that on which the first copy of the charter was sealed, although the process of issue took several weeks thereafter, as further copies, perhaps as many as forty, were prepared and sent out to be proclaimed in the individual English county courts. Copies were still being distributed as late as 22 July. The dating clause also demonstrates a desire to define what was clearly an unfamiliar place of issue. Similar clauses are to be found at the end of other medieval peace treaties. Indeed, they are a means of distinguishing peace treaties from other documentary types, as things negotiated in liminal spaces, lying neither in one location nor another but at a meeting point between two territorial

powers. Henry II's treaty with Philip Augustus in 1180, for
example, had been issued 'Between Gisors and Trie'; King
Richard's in 1195 'Between Gaillon and Vaudreuil'. But for this
peculiarity of diplomatic practice, the very name 'Runnymede'
might be as unfamiliar to us today as it must have been to those
who met there in the early summer of 1215. A contemporary,
translating Magna Carta into Anglo-Norman French, was
so bemused by the name that he rendered it in the wholly
unintelligible form 'Roueninkmede'.

In format and in the language of its opening and closing
formulae, Magna Carta remained a royal charter. It was granted
by the king, dated by his regnal year, and sealed with his royal
seal (we do not need here to rehearse the old caution against
assuming that John 'signed' Magna Carta). Albeit that it included
some bizarre variations on accepted practice, claiming to be
granted first and foremost to God, and under its 'security' clause
(clause 61) nominating a committee of twenty-five barons to
police its permanent enforcement, these in themselves offered no
real protection. As a royal charter, issued with the king's assent,
Magna Carta could be repudiated as soon as such assent was
withdrawn. Previous peace treaties, not least those between
England and France, had been accompanied by the most solemn
of guarantees. None of this had prevented kings, whenever it
suited them, from breaking their treaties and re-opening
hostilities. A treaty of 1163, for example, negotiated between
Henry II of England and the count of Flanders (one of the few
such treaties whose precise text has come down to us), contained
detailed provision for twelve guarantors from each side to act as
'hostages', liable to fixed financial penalties if the terms of the
treaty were breached. The total number of twenty-four
guarantors, with the king or the count at their head, brings us to
something very close to the number twenty-five so significant in
Magna Carta. The 1163 treaty itself had been repudiated the
moment when the Flemings realized the advantages to be gained
by siding with the baronial rebels of 1173.

4. King John 'signing' Magna Carta, as imagined by a 19th-century print-maker

The king remained a free agent, however severe the limitations his subjects might seek to impose upon his exercise of free will. As a result, as King John was to prove within only two months of the Runnymede settlement, no royal charter was inviolable. By September 1215, with most of its terms still unfulfilled, Magna Carta was a dead letter. The barons had once again thrown off their homage and made war on the king, garrisoning Rochester Castle (the gateway to London) against him. The king himself had sent requests to Rome both that Magna Carta be annulled (an annulment that Pope Innocent III was only too happy to supply) and that the rebels and their clerical supporters, up to and including Stephen Langton, be excommunicated and suspended from office. To this extent, Magna Carta in its original form never took effect. It was a peace treaty that brought not peace but war.

Its terms are themselves a bizarre combination of the over-general and what can seem the excessively precise. For those today who speak of Magna Carta as the foundation stone of democracy, what, for example, are we to make of clause 33 ('Henceforth all fish-weirs will be completely removed from the Thames and the Medway'), or clause 50 ('We shall dismiss completely from their offices the relations of Girard d'Athée...namely Engelard de Cigogné, Peter, Guy and Andrew de Chanceaux, Guy de Cigogné, Geoffrey de Martigny with his brothers (and) Philip Mark....')? For an English constitution supposedly founded upon principles of tolerance and asylum, what are we to make of the xenophobic clause 51, promising the expulsion of all 'alien knights, crossbowmen, serjeants and mercenaries who have come with horses and arms to the injury of the realm'? In the circumstances of 1215 such precision made perfect sense. Fish weirs slowed the navigation of rivers and therefore posed a threat to inland trade. The navigation of the Thames and the Medway had been specifically guaranteed in royal charters to the men of London since at least the 1190s. The kinsmen of Girard d'Athée were amongst those exiles from John's lands in France promoted to the custody of castles and sheriffdoms. In the summer of 1215, these were the constables and sheriffs who posed greatest threat to the rebel barons. Their names may be unfamiliar today, just as at the time the barons had difficulty in distinguishing between one Johnny foreigner and another: Guy de Chanceaux for example, is almost certainly the same man as Guy de Cigogné, mistakenly given a double identity in Magna Carta. Yet at least one man on this list, Philip Mark, is still a notorious (if nameless) figure today. Philip was King John's sheriff of Nottingham, the archetype for the later villain of the Robin Hood legends.

Much of the second half of Magna Carta is given over to specifics: clauses 56–8, for example, on peace with Wales intended to deprive the barons of Welsh assistance; clause 59, intended to ensure a similar peace on John's northern frontiers with Scotland. Other matters were left deliberately vague. Clauses 52 and 55, for example, defer any decision in specific disputes, over land or money, to adjudication by the baronial twenty-five, and in the case of clause 55, by Archbishop Langton. Clause 53 delays any decision on the destruction or retention of forests until the king's return from Crusade: a Crusade on which John had little real intention of embarking, even though it is mentioned again in clause 52, to reiterate the degree to which the king, as a vowed Crusader, enjoyed the protection of the Church.

Elsewhere, although the charter touches upon matters of profound and general rather than local or temporary significance, the principles it establishes are so imprecise as to suggest deliberate caution on behalf of those who drafted it. What, for example, in any precise sense, were the 'rights' and 'liberties' of the English Church guaranteed in clause 1? Who were the 'peers' of clause 39, whose judgment alone could lead to the outlawry of free men? What, in any case, constituted 'lawful judgment'? Above all, given that there was no written code of laws that applied throughout England or that was officially recognized as royal law, how was anyone to determine whether a judgment had been delivered in accordance with 'the law of the land' (clause 39, the most famous though also one of the vaguest of clauses)? Modern lawyers would drive a coach and horses through such imprecision. Indeed, the meaning of individual clauses was to be debated for many years after 1215. When the charter demanded (clause 6) that heirs be married 'without disparagement', it was to take fifty years before 'disparagement' was precisely defined, not just as marriage to someone of lower status but specifically to those of foreign birth. When clause 7 referred to a widow's 'dower', it was not for a further ten years that dower itself was defined as one-third of a husband's lands, and even then there were to be problems in enforcing this as a universal practice, not least in the city of London where local custom, potentially allowing a widow far less, was still being upheld thirty years later.

The first thing that should be apparent from the text (and, once again, readers are urged to read through the individual clauses), is that, for all its emphasis upon the 'law of the land' or 'law of the realm' (mentioned as guiding principles in clauses 39, 42, 45, 55, more frequently than any other concept save for the 'reason' or 'reasonableness' cited in clauses 4, 5, 12, 15, 26, 29), this was not a textbook codification of English law. Despite the fact that it was in their jurisdiction over crime that king and barons most frequently came into contact with 'the law' as we would today understand it, Magna Carta has virtually nothing to say of criminal procedures save for general references to outlawry in clause 39. It should also be apparent that a very large part of the document relates to the financial relations between the king as lord and his barons as subjects. Feudal 'incidents' (the payments owed to lords and exploited to the utmost by lords seeking to profit from lordship) loom particularly large. Not only does the charter reiterate, and in some cases clarify, the restrictions on such payments already set out in Henry I's coronation charter of 1100, but it enters into details here to a degree not found when it turns to more general legal principles. Thus, after what was clearly considerable debate (clause 2), it specifies the 'relief' paid at the inheritance of an earl or a baron as £100, and that paid by a knight as 100 shillings (£5). In clauses

3–5, defining what a lord might or might not take as 'reasonable' profits from wardship of an under-age heir, there is a determination to cover all eventualities, for example (clause 5) by reference to 'houses, parks, fishponds, ponds, mills....ploughs and wainage (i.e. carts)' amongst the property to be protected. Throughout, the emphasis upon what is 'reasonable' is yet further proof of the degree to which law and good lordship were themselves linked to the concept of rationality. Irrationality, by contrast, was equated with sinfulness and with lordship that was bad.

Most of the first half of the charter, and more than half of its clauses all told, are concerned with precisely those areas in which King John and his Exchequer had abused privileges of lordship that might be deemed either 'reasonable' or 'customary'. Thus, there are clauses dealing with inheritance and wardship (clauses 2–5); marriage and widowhood (clauses 6–8); debt and its collection (clauses 9–11, 26–7, including debt owed to Jews); scutage, aid, and taxation (clauses 12–13, 15); lordship over fees and churches (clauses 32, 46); service including that owed for knights, castles, and for the county farms, as well as obligations to build bridges or supply corn or foodstuffs, horses and carts, and building materials (clauses 16, 23, 28–31, 37, 43); the forests (clauses 44, 47–8, 53); the profits of justice (clauses 20–2); and the particular mercantile regulations of the city of London and other towns (clauses 13, 33, 35, 41–2). Even clauses 10–11, that to a modern audience might be read as evidence of medieval anti-Semitism, respond to the fact that, in feudal terms, the Jews were the king's personal possessions, those owing money to them ultimately owing such debts to the king. Both John before 1215 and the barons after their seizure of London had deliberately attacked the Jews, in order to profit from their money-lending or, in the case of the barons, to destroy all evidence of it, not first and foremost out of religious, let alone race, hatred.

Besides restricting the king's profits from feudal 'incidents', and defining what might constitute real necessity for a lord to take an

'aid' or compulsory tax from his free men (clauses 12 and 15,
allowing only three such obligations, to ransom a lord's body, to
pay for the knighting of his eldest son, and the marriage of his
eldest daughter), a significant number of the charter's clauses are
given over not so much to the principles as to the procedures of
the law. Once again, this reflects a situation in which, as overlord,
the king was suspected of manipulating the law courts to increase
his own lordly profits. Thus, besides the general prohibitions
against arbitrary accusations (clause 38), judgments (clauses 39),
and the sale of justice (clause 40), there are clauses restricting the
judicial powers of sheriffs (clause 24) and insisting that the most
frequently sought procedures to reclaim inheritance or land or
rights to the patronage of churches (clause 18) be available
speedily and locally. Clause 17, although interpreted later as
providing for a permanent court at Westminster known as 'The
Bench', was in fact a response to King John's failure to send out
regular visitations of justices to the counties (the so-called 'eyre').
The intention here was to ensure that justice in 'common pleas'
(that is, pleas involving the king's universal, public, or 'common'
jurisdiction) be speedily obtainable, either at Westminster or in
the regular visitations that the Westminster justices made via the
'eyre'. Litigants and jurors were no longer to be forced to track the
uncertain movements of the king's itinerant court. Clause 34 deals
with the fear that a particular type of writ (named 'Praecipe', after
its opening instruction to the local sheriff, 'Order that...') might
be used to deprive barons of their jurisdiction over disputes that
otherwise were being sued in the king's rather than in the local
baronial court.

In hindsight, and despite what at first glance can seem an
overwhelming quantity of 'feudal' detail, we find much here of
principle, significant to future relations between sovereign and
people. Over tax, for example, the charter insisted that, beyond
the three cases of necessity that were specifically allowed, no king
might arbitrarily tax his subjects without first obtaining their
consent. Consent itself was here (clause 14) interpreted to mean a

properly summoned representative assembly both of the greater and the lesser tenants of the king, in essence a meeting not dissimilar to those that by the 1230s were named 'parliaments' ('talkings together') and that thereafter proved increasingly resistant to royal demands for tax. It was this combination of tax strike and insistence upon the right to consultation that was to lead, from the 1250s onwards, to a formalized 'Parliament' with a capital 'P': a public gathering where kings and representatives of the realm might meet.

The idea of government conducted on behalf of the 'community of the realm' was likewise, in the 1250s and 1260s, to dominate political debate. This too could trace a descent from the demand by Magna Carta, clause 61, that in forcing the king to obey his undertakings the baronial committee of twenty-five be assisted by the 'commune of the whole land'. In the French version of the 1215 charter, apparently distributed for reading in the shires, this phrase was translated more potently still as 'the community of all England' (the *commune de tote Engleterre*). Magna Carta, clause 60, insisting that the privileges of the few be extended to the many, although modelled upon Henry I's coronation charter, represents a significant step towards the recognition of public good, rather than the personal advantage of the king, as the chief purpose of the law: no longer merely the Roman imperial principle, 'What pleases the prince has the force of law', but a step towards the formulation, itself borrowed from the Roman writer Cicero, 'Let the supreme law be the welfare of the people'.

Little of this would have been apparent to those who in the summer of 1215 attempted to implement the uneasy peace that Magna Carta secured. Required to dismiss his alien constables, the king delayed. Requested, as a reciprocal gesture, to surrender possession of the Tower of London, the barons refused. Expected, as a supposedly neutral mediator, to shuttle between king and barons, Archbishop Langton lost the confidence of both parties and, for his refusal to surrender Rochester Castle, earned the undying mistrust of the king. In his letters demanding Rochester's surrender, the king pleaded 'necessity' (the condition that Langton had himself accepted as the chief justification of royal policy), to which Langton replied with a demand for proper 'judgment', citing the language of Magna Carta, clause 39. Having solemnly promised, according to clause 61 of Magna Carta, to 'procure nothing from anyone...by which any of these concessions and liberties will be revoked or diminished', within a month the king had appealed to the pope. The pope, having already excommunicated the rebels, on 24 August 1215, issued letters freeing John from his oaths and declaring the charter itself shameful, demeaning, unjust, and, because extracted by force, hereby annulled. These letters took more than a month to reach England, but papal excommunication of the rebels and the king's rejection of all previous baronial constitutions was already announced on 4 September. By 17 September, the king was once again ordering the seizure of rebel lands. The barons wrote to France inviting Louis, son of King Philip, to become their king. Peace dissolved into civil war. A French army occupied London. John himself ruled little save for a militarized enclave in the English south-west. Magna Carta, the treaty that failed, was consigned to oblivion. Within nine weeks of its issue, it was to all intents and purposes redundant: so much scrap parchment for rats to nibble at.

Yet it survived. In October 1216, in the midst of civil war, John attempted to cross the Lincolnshire estuary known as the Wash. Taken unawares by the tide, he lost much of his baggage and perhaps a considerable quantity of his treasure. He himself fell ill at Newark, where he sickened and died. He left a nine-year-old boy, his son, Henry III, as heir to the throne, crowned king by a papal legate with the approval of only a small rump of John's former courtiers. The coronation was held at Gloucester, in the greatest haste, clearly for fear that if the royalists did not move swiftly, Louis of France might be crowned in the rightful coronation church, Westminster Abbey, controlled by the rebel barons. Gloucester Abbey, where the coronation took place, was a site long associated with English kingship, close both to Worcester, where John had requested burial, and to Bristol, the principal royal garrison in the west. Above all, it was a church dedicated to St Peter, the first of the popes, to whom Westminster was also dedicated. This was to be a ceremony that advertised the pope's protection for the new king, orphaned and a child. To broadcast their determination to rule differently from King John, the guardians of Henry III now revived the great charter of June 1215, reissuing it at Bristol in November 1216, no longer as an assault upon royal privilege but as a manifesto of future good government.

The Runnymede treaty of 1215 expired within nine weeks, rejected by king and pope. From its wreckage, there now emerged something entirely different: a coronation charter for Henry III, far more substantial than any previous coronation charter because dictated by circumstances far more perilous. In the process, whilst the legal and administrative clauses of 1215 were preserved, most of the more controversial matter was jettisoned: no security clause, no insistence upon the dismissal of the king's alien constables, no baronial committee of twenty-five, a watering-down of the provisions to summon councils of greater and lesser tenants. Amid civil war, there was also a greater emphasis upon castles, not least in clauses guaranteeing the rights of widows who were now to be protected against the possibility that their chief residence might be a castle, and hence unsuitable lodgings after the death of a husband. This was now a charter, not a treaty. More significant than any rewriting, the charter reissued at Bristol was not simply sealed with the royal seal, revocable at the king's will. Instead, since the boy king had no seal, it was sealed by the king's chief minister, William Marshal, and by the papal legate, the Italian Guala Bicchieri. In lending his, and hence the pope's, authority to the document, the legate transformed Magna Carta into a papally authorized settlement. Henceforth, it would be very

5. King John, from his tomb effigy at Worcester

difficult, for any pope as for any king, to annul. England's liberties were won from a nine-year-old Angevin king, provoked by a French invasion, and confirmed under the seal of an Italian cardinal. So much for the idea of the English constitution as something isolated from continental politics, immunized against European influence.

As in all previous baronial rebellions, the balance of power tipped overwhelmingly in favour of royal authority, even though that authority was vested in a nine-year-old boy. Henry III's regime not only survived but inflicted a series of military defeats upon the rebels, most notably in a great battle fought at Lincoln in May 1217. Three months later, as the result of a naval engagement fought off the coast of Kent, French reinforcements were dispatched to the depths of the English Channel. It was the rebels rather than the royalists who now sued for peace. As a token of royal magnanimity and of the boy king's determination to rule in peace and harmony with his barons, Magna Carta was reissued, in November 1217, with minor changes to the text of 1216, sealed by both the king's guardian and the papal legate. The reissue of 1217 was accompanied by the grant of a Charter of the Forests: a subsidiary series of clauses dealing with those issues of forest law which, in the original settlement of 1215, had been set aside for future discussion. It was in order to distinguish between the principal charter of liberties and this new Forest Charter that, as early as 1218, contemporaries began to refer to the charter of liberties as the 'great' or 'Magna' Carta.

Strangled at birth in the summer of 1215, Magna Carta was thus resurrected both in 1216 and 1217, with the explicit support of the Church. Henceforth, not only the English bishops but the pope ranked amongst its principal sponsors. Not all of King Henry III's courtiers were so enthusiastic. The forester, William Brewer, suggested that Magna Carta was best consigned to oblivion. The bishop of Winchester, Peter des Roches, spent much of the next twenty years attempting to restore royal government to the arbitrary authority that it had enjoyed under King John. Nevertheless, in the country at large, Magna Carta had already begun to acquire totemic status as a touchstone of communal liberties guaranteeing the king's subjects against tyranny. In 1225, desperate for a grant of taxation, Henry III once again confirmed the charter, sending exemplifications into each of the English shires. Whatever his role in the initial settlement of 1215, Stephen

6. Magna Carta 1217 sealed by William Marshal (right) and the legate Guala (left)

Langton, still archbishop of Canterbury, was a moving force behind this third reissue. Once again, this was a settlement clearly linked to European concerns. The king needed tax both to pay for the recovery of his English castles from foreign mercenaries, and to prop up what little remained of his continental empire, shaken by a French assault on Poitou and the great port of La Rochelle.

Henceforth, it was the 1225 Magna Carta and its accompanying Forest Charter that became the standard texts enshrined in law. Pared down from the more than sixty clauses of 1215 to a bare thirty-seven, Magna Carta had completed its metamorphosis from peace settlement into legislation. Pressure from the county communities, from the knights of the shire and from those whose careers were passed largely outside the confines of the royal court, led to yet further reissues during the next seventy years. In 1234, for example, after a period in which Peter des Roches had sought to restore many of the arbitrary devices of King John, Henry III guaranteed to uphold Magna Carta as a means of signalling his breach with the controversial policies of his minister. The crisis of 1234 had itself been provoked by attempts to revoke earlier charters granted by John or Henry III to particular barons. Henceforth, it was recognized that no king could arbitrarily repeal or revoke his own charters without fundamentally destabilizing the political community. Magna Carta was thus even further guaranteed against attack.

All told, between 1225 and Henry III's death in 1272, the king promised on nearly a dozen occasions to uphold the 'charters of liberties', meaning Magna Carta and the Forest Charter. From the 1250s, we read of the charter being proclaimed not only in the Latin of the clergy but in baronial French and in the English of the common people. Just such a trilingual proclamation is first implied by letters sent out by papal commissioners in the autumn of 1255. Once again, it is instructive to find the Church, and indeed the pope, so prominent not only in the preservation but in the continued proclamation of the charter. This was a document that declared the liberty of the Church. As such, it was now assured ecclesiastical protection. Elevated to that hallowed atmosphere in which the Church guarded its most precious relics, it was nonetheless broadcast with the Church's approval in the same language in which ordinary men and women bought their bread or gossiped with their neighbours.

In 1215, 1216, 1217, 1225 and again in 1265, when the 1225 charter was reissued at the height of yet another baronial rebellion, effectively with the king under close arrest, we have certain proof that the text of Magna Carta was sent into the English localities under the king's own seal. For the most part, the king's commitments to uphold Magna Carta involved not a full distribution of the charter but the issue of letters promising renewal and respect for its terms. By the 1220s, indeed, there was already uncertainty over the status of the various reissues. The chroniclers of St Albans Abbey, Roger of Wendover and Matthew Paris, added to the confusion here, for partisan ends deliberately popularizing a hybrid version combining elements of the 1215 and the 1225 Magna Cartas. In general, it was the 1225 version that was reported and recorded in the registers of writs and statutes that increasingly became the textbooks of legal students and professional lawyers. Even here, there was uncertainty. In 1297, when again in return for taxation and the settlement of grievances, Edward I, King John's grandson, granted a full reissue of the 1225 charter, the text chosen for confirmation seems to have been taken from just such an unofficial lawyer's collection. Although in theory a simple recital of the text of 1225, the 1297 Magna Carta includes a subtle change to clause 2, demanding that an earl pay a relief of £100 to inherit, but that a baron pay merely 100 marks (£66). Just such a distinction seems to have been discussed but rejected during the negotiations of 1215. It was now reintroduced, more than eighty years later, as the result of careless copying. Because Edward I was in Flanders when the 1297 charter was issued by his councillors, under the king's seal of absence, there was a final reissue of Magna Carta in 1300, now once again distributed to the counties and cathedrals of England under the king's great seal. This was the last. Although, thereafter, Magna Carta was 'confirmed' more than forty times during the course of the next two hundred years, such confirmations involved promises to uphold its terms, not a physical distribution of copies to the country at large.

Magna Carta had been sent into Ireland as early as 1216. Durham, which claimed to stand outside the ordinary jurisdiction of the kings of England, seems to have accepted the charter from the outset. Perhaps precisely because of their jurisdictional peculiarities, it was the monks of Durham who proved most assiduous in guarding Magna Carta in each of its successive issues. 'Originals' of the issues of 1216, 1225, and 1300 are still in the Durham archives. By contrast, the county of Cheshire, ruled by its local earl, seems not fully to have accepted Magna Carta into the 1230s, even though in 1215 or 1216 the earl of Chester had issued his own 'Cheshire Magna Carta', rehearsing some of the charter's principles but combining them with provisions of purely local significance. An early French translation of the 1215 charter made its way into Normandy, where it was considered of sufficient interest to be copied by the authorities of the hospital at Pont-Audemer.

By the 1290s, there is evidence for a more general Norman interest in Magna Carta: an attempt, indeed, by various Norman lawyers to suggest that the 1225 Magna Carta had been granted not by King Henry III but by his grandfather, Henry II. As such, so the argument seems to have run, it should be applied to Normandy and to those who were otherwise governed by the laws of the kings of France. This deception was made all the easier by the fact that, after the French conquest of 1204, Normandy was soon awash with charters purporting to have been issued by earlier English kings, granting liberties which the new French conquerors found very difficult to deny. The earliest collection of specifically Norman law, the so-called *Très Ancien Coutumier*, is itself infused with principles and practices so similar to those of Magna Carta that either we must conclude that Magna Carta derived significant input from Norman law or, as now seems more likely, that the *Très Ancien Coutumier*, first recorded c. 1300, was itself deeply influenced by the 1225 Magna Carta. This would make sense, since the study of Norman law, and the emergence of Norman resistance to French taxation, culminated, in March 1315, with the issue by Louis X, King of France, of a 'Charte aux normands': in effect, a great charter of liberties for the Norman people guaranteeing the independence of their legal system almost exactly a century after Runnymede. Some of the laws of medieval Normandy still have effect in the Channel Islands. We are therefore confronted with the delicious paradox that those parts of the United Kingdom today keenest to guard their independence from English statute – the states (and with them the offshore investment trusts) of Guernsey and Jersey – do so on the basis of medieval Norman customary law itself infused with the spirit of England's Magna Carta. Magna Carta was by 1300 already launched upon its international career, as a totem not just for the English but for anyone else seeking to share in English 'liberties'.

As the crude rewritings of the 'Norman' Magna Carta suggest, the charter's celebrity increased even whilst its precise historical meaning faded from memory. By the time of its last full reissue in England, in 1300, much of the text of Magna Carta had become an anachronism. New priorities now governed disputes between the king and his critics, in particular the king's demands for tax and for the right to 'purveyance' (forced seizures for the needs of war) which were only inadequately covered by the terms of Magna Carta. Hence, as early as 1300, the issue of a series of supplementary 'Articles over the Charter', intended to clarify and to extend the provisions of the 1220s, themselves no longer deemed fit for purpose.

The charter itself continued to be confirmed, on numerous occasions in the 14th century, mostly in response to parliamentary petitions. Most involved public proclamation by the king and his ministers of their agreement to uphold the charter's terms. Often, this was linked to parliamentary votes of taxation, or referred to specific liberties that Parliament and its petitioners wished to see enforced: over the freedom of the Church, over purveyance, over forced labour services, over particular local interests including the navigation of the Thames, or the claims of individual barons to protection from the consequences of wardship or debt. As this should remind us, Magna Carta was more often cited for its protection of individuals, ultimately as a 'selfish' baronial instrument, than in defence of the community at large. This tension, between private and public interest, remains a feature of its use even today. In the modern American Supreme Court, for example, Magna Carta has been more often cited in defence of individual property-holders and the rights of corporations against the federal government than in defence of the community against private or corporate self-interest.

Parliament's role in the confirmation of Magna Carta introduces us to a further paradox. Magna Carta was intended to place limitations upon the sovereign powers of the king. As early as 1369, however, in passing legislation intended to ensure that no-one in future might alter or amend the charter's terms, Parliament in effect laid claim to authority over and above the charter. This was a two-edged weapon, since if one Parliament sought to protect Magna Carta, what was to prevent a subsequent Parliament from claiming the power to amend or even annul it?

None of this was immediately apparent. It was the threat of royal rather than parliamentary sovereignty that continued to vex those who had dealings with Magna Carta into the 15th and 16th centuries. Although by now virtually redundant as law, superceded or contradicted by subsequent statutes, Magna Carta remained the first item in the statute books: the venerable and bewhiskered Genesis prefacing the common body of knowledge that most lawyers possessed. It was in this capacity, as a legislative relic, that it was first published, following the introduction of the printing press, in a series of statute books, beginning with a Latin text of the 1300 charter in 1508, and thereafter proceeding via a (crabbed and inaccurate) English translation in 1534. In Shakespeare's play of *King John* (c. 1595), there is no mention of Magna Carta, even though tyranny is the central theme with which Shakespeare deals. We have seen already that arguments based upon antiquity, necessity, and rationality were crucial to the circumstances in which the charter was first issued. These same issues were to resurface towards the end of the 16th century. Thus Magna Carta remained at the centre of the political stage: a venerable actor from the past whose longevity was prized above all other aspects of performance and whose retirement the public simply refused to allow.

Chapter 6
The charter as totem and as artefact

In the struggles between Parliament and the Stuart kings after 1600, Magna Carta played a distinguished part. In the hands of lawyers such as Sir Edward Coke and John Hampden its chief role was to serve as an embodiment of an 'Ancient Constitution' imperilled by the Stuart drive towards absolutism. In the 12th and 13th centuries, kings had claimed not so much to make new laws as to confirm the old, so that the coronation charter of Henry I claimed merely to restate the laws of Edward the Confessor. In the same way, to the lawyers of the 17th century the idea of the law as something ancient and immutable, tampered with only at the nation's peril, was central to the defence of the rights of subjects against the king. Coke implied that aspects of the ancient constitution, not least Parliament itself, were as old as King Arthur, perhaps as old as the city of Troy from which Arthur's forebears had supposedly fled to England. This was nonsense. It nonetheless threw a spotlight on Magna Carta as an embodiment of good old law, hallowed by time yet now endangered.

As in many situations in which historical records are placed at the service of lawyers, there was considerable tension here between fact and interpretation. No-one in the 17th century had a proper understanding of Magna Carta's history. Many depended upon the texts transmitted by the chroniclers of St Albans, in which the 1215 and 1225 charters were hopelessly confused. Lawyers used the 1225 text whilst supposing that they dealt with a charter granted by John. The fact that Magna Carta itself had undergone a series of transformations between 1215 and 1225 was, to say the least, inconvenient to any argument that the constitution was of its nature unchanging and unalterable. John's chief crime, in the eyes of Shakespeare, as of most English historians, was his craven surrender of England to the pope. Magna Carta, although supported by Stephen Langton, a cardinal of the Roman Church, and subsequently preserved by popes and papal legates, was presented to the 17th century as a Protestant manifesto: a defence of the religious as well as the 'feudal' liberties of freeborn Englishmen.

Nonetheless, the idea of a charter of liberties, embodying the subject's rights against the sovereign, took deep root. It underlies not only the various parliamentary experiments to impeach the king's ministers and to produce 'remonstrances' against bad government, but the chartered privileges which kings themselves continued to grant, not least to the fledgling American colonies. Coke played a part in drafting the first charter of the Virginia Company in 1606, promising colonists 'all liberties, franchises and immunities . . . as if they had been abiding and born within this our realm of England'. The liberties of Englishmen were similarly guaranteed in the charters of Massachusetts (1629), Maryland (1632), Connecticut (1662), Rhode Island and Carolina (both 1663), and Georgia (1732). In this way, and by grace of precisely those Stuart kings, James I and Charles I, who were elsewhere accused of suborning the ancient constitution, Magna Carta and the principles of English liberty were exported across the north Atlantic just as previously they had been exported to Ireland and Normandy.

It was not only the parliamentary opposition but the king himself who appealed to ancient law and privilege. The debates over Ship Money in the 1630s, in which Magna Carta was cited, were inspired by Charles I's revival of a number of 'feudal' taxes and obligations. In just this way, Charles sought to reassert rights over the royal forests which in times past had been allowed to lapse. Magna Carta was cited during the impeachment of the king's ministers, Strafford in 1641 and Laud in 1645. It supplied a model for the Grand Remonstrance against royal government in 1641. In wider terms, there are obvious parallels to be drawn between the armed uprising of the peers and parliamentarians in the 1640s and that of the barons in the 1170s or in 1215. As on both of those previous occasions, fear was by no means the least significant of policy-makers. It was fear of King John in 1212 that led his barons to plot assassination. It was fear of Charles I that in 1649 led to his beheading. Not everyone agreed the precise significance of Magna Carta. Indeed, as we have seen, as a guide to lawyers or the devisers of law, there was much about Magna Carta that was far too vague or anachronistic for present use. Nonetheless, in the 1680s, as in the 1640s, when England rose against a Stuart king and expelled the hapless James II, it was Magna Carta that was cited as a model for the Bill of Rights (1689), an 'Act Declaring the Rights and Liberties of the Subject and Settling the Succession of the Crown'.

This reference to 'rights' is itself significant and reflects a notable change in thinking. Against the early Stuarts, Magna Carta was cited as an embodiment of the 'Ancient Constitution', conceived of as something historically tangible: a brake applied by the past to present tendencies within the law. The more, however, that historians searched for that shaggiest of beasts, the ancient and immutable constitution, the less substantial its carcass appeared to be. Coke's successors found themselves not so much in a liberal Elysium of natural laws and freedoms as in some terrible forerunner of Jurassic Park, excavating the remains of a still-breathing and distinctly carnivorous monster: the absolute sovereignty of the king. As early as the 1620s, the greatest of the Stuart historians, Henry Spelman, had come to realize that the 'parliaments' which first appeared in 13th-century sources were baronial affairs, meetings of lords rather than 'Commons'.

Spelman's discoveries here were not published until the 1660s, by which time William Prynne had toiled in the archives to prove that no summons to county and borough representatives was known earlier than 1265. It was left to the irascible Cambridge medic Robert Brady, writing in the 1670s, to assert not only that the 'councils' of the centuries on either side of the Norman Conquest were baronial affairs, attended principally by bishops, earls, and barons, but that the 'Commons' had no real existence before the reign of Edward I. For the first seventy years of its recorded existence, Parliament had no proper tradition of 'elected' members, no properly established body equivalent to the later House of Commons, and few functions other than to assent to and lend public authority to decisions already reached by the king. Magna Carta was in essence no more than a royal charter, an exercise of the sovereign's grace. Parliament, once regarded as Magna Carta's coadjutor, was likewise a king's invention, in its earliest years a mere theatre for the display of royal magnanimity.

With Parliament itself now unmasked as a royal bastard, the past no longer applied any sure brake upon the king's sovereignty. Moreover, from the 1680s, the threat of tyranny increasingly came not from a monarchy weakened by successive rebellions and revolutions, but from Parliament's own claims to sovereign privilege. Arguments more effective than mere antiquity had to be devised to protect the liberties of Englishmen. Oliver Cromwell, chief architect of the most violent of the 17th-century revolutions, informed as Lord Protector that he was acting contrary to Magna Carta, is said to have replied that 'their Magna Farta should not control his actions'. Gerard Winstanley, most radical of the reformers, perceived as early as the 1640s that Magna Carta was no more than a royal act of grace, defending the rights of only a small minority of property-holders. Into the position previously occupied by the ancient constitution, there now stepped the idea of 'natural law': fundamental legal principles transcending mere historical circumstance. In fact, there was little new here. We have found, as early as King John's reign, the appeal both to 'necessity' and to 'reason' as fundamental principles underlying the negotiation of Magna Carta. Both terms, 'necessity' and 'reason', were germane to the 17th and 18th centuries, albeit now to a large extent divorced from the scriptural or theological imperatives that had once been assumed to govern their operation. The rights to which theorists such as John Locke aspired, and ultimately the *Rights of Man* (1791) that Tom Paine declared should supercede any feudal relic such as Magna Carta, were not that far removed from the 'necessities' or 'reason' with which 13th-century theorists had sought to control the otherwise irrational propensities of kingship.

All of this should have consigned Magna Carta to oblivion. It did not. Exhibiting that fondness for the homespun which is an abiding feature of English law, those who in the 18th century attempted to challenge Parliament, for example by resisting arrest for so-called 'seditious libels', did so with Magna Carta clutched firmly in their hands. Almost literally so in the case of Arthur Beardmore in 1762 and Sir Francis Burdett in 1810, both of whom contrived, at the times of their arrest, to be found teaching Magna Carta to their sons. Quite what these boys made of their lessons is not recorded, but the images of them circulated via cheap prints gave a powerful impression of Magna Carta as something akin to holy writ: a 'bible' of liberty in an age of godless libertines.

In the debates over the American colonies, stirred up by Parliament's claims to tax the colonists, Edmund Burke demanded that settlers in America have the same liberties as Englishmen and therefore 'sit down...to the feast of Magna Charta'. The principle of 'No taxation without representation' itself could claim roots in Magna Carta, clause 14, with its demand for 'common counsel' before tax was granted. In 1770, there were calls for a committee of twenty-five barons to sit in judgment upon King George III. In the following year, we find the first of many proposals that

7. Arthur Beardmore teaching Magna Carta to his son

15 June, the anniversary of Magna Carta, be set aside as 'a day of public thanksgiving, festivity and joy'.

For those, on the other side of the debate, who sought to assert the sovereignty not of the people but of king or Parliament, Magna Carta remained equally useful. Indeed, it was Sir William Blackstone's attempt to justify parliamentary sovereignty on the basis of 'necessity' (the need for a sovereign power to keep all competing authorities in check) that first led him to Magna Carta. It was Blackstone's edition of 1759 that for the first time drew a proper distinction between Magna Carta 1215 and the reissue of 1225, the text generally cited in law. Given the ensuing revolutions in America and France, a fear emerged that, however 'natural' they might be, the 'Rights of Man' threatened to ride roughshod over both reason and tradition. Those seeking to protect society against chaos argued that repression was itself a 'necessity' to preserve the constitution and ancient law against furious and desperate men. Meanwhile, Magna Carta entered the debates over reform of the British Parliament.

By this time, it is very doubtful whether even its keenest advocates had read it or knew any of its terms, beyond perhaps the general defence of lawful judgment in clauses 39 and 40. Rather like those workers of the industrial north who in the 1820s demanded 'Universal Suffrage' on the understanding that this meant that if one person suffered then so should everyone else, citation of Magna Carta tended to be crude and anachronistic. Thomas Macaulay, England's greatest historian and an active Whig politician, referred in the reform debates of the early 1830s to the Reform Bill as 'a greater charter of the liberties of England', deliberately placing it in succession to the charter of 1215. In the same way, the 'People's Charter' of the 1830s and 1840s, the object for which the 'Chartists' struggled, was presented as a latter-day version of the settlement agreed at Runnymede.

In the American courts, Magna Carta continued to be cited as the inheritance of a legal system itself in part derived from English common law. Even on the European Continent, gripped by Anglomania as a result of Wellington's victories, keen to discover the recipe for England's avoidance of revolutionary bloodshed, Magna Carta (in French 'La Grande Charte'), was not forgotten. France acquired a 'Charter' as a result of the restoration of Louis XVIII in 1814, with deliberate echoes of the limitations that Magna Carta had placed upon royal excess. Central to political debates under the Bourbon monarchy, it was revised as a result of the French revolution of 1830, and inspired the adoption of a similar 'Charte Constitutionelle' for the new kingdom of Belgium, itself one of the outcomes of the chaos of 1830. At the same time, the principal scholarly institution in France established to study and catalogue the evidence of the medieval past was named the École des Chartes ('The Charters School'), permanently established in Paris in 1829, and still one of the French *grandes écoles*, responsible for the education of archivists and librarians.

The irony is that these homages to Magna Carta were paid at almost precisely the time that the charter itself began to fade from law into history. Two processes were crucial here. The first was law reform. Since the 17th century, it had been apparent that English law was a tangled thicket of statute and precedent. Successive statutes or acts of Parliament had altered or superceded earlier legislation without any attempt to repeal or codify the pre-existing laws thus rendered obsolete. There was no official statute book, merely a series of semi-official collections circulating amongst lawyers, claiming varying degrees of reliability or comprehensiveness. There was nothing especially English about this chaos. Save for the popes, who had sponsored digests of canon law since the 12th century, and for Sicily where there were attempts at codification in the 1220s, few European states could claim that their laws were properly published, let alone understood. Despite precocious moves by the authorities of Bavaria (1756) and Prussia (1794), it was the French Revolution that brought fundamental change, setting France on the road to the standardization of law.

Not until 1810, and even then only as a result of competition with the French Code Napoléon of 1804, was there an official attempt to publish the laws of England. The nine vast folios of these *Statutes of the Realm* began, naturally enough, with Magna Carta 1215. They also revealed the degree to which the laws of England were inconsistent, self-contradictory, riddled with textual confusions, and weighed down with medieved anachronisms. Beginning in the 1820s, and ironically enough spurred on by the success of Napoleon, England's old enemy, in imposing order upon the laws of France, attempts were made to codify English criminal law, where some of the worst abuses lay. As law-makers strained to grasp the realities of the modern industrial state, a more general reform of the law, including repeal of redundant legislation, became an urgent necessity.

A second great spur to change came from a new historical understanding. It is no coincidence that this change occurred at precisely the same time that scientists and textual critics began to question whether the Bible and other religious texts could any longer be accepted as history rather than as metaphor. Neither the laws of old England nor those revealed by the Bible, it now came to be realized, were necessarily unalterable. As with codification, much of this new thinking was imported from France and Germany, whose scholars were already insisting that the documentary sources for the past be properly published and contextualized. Thanks to a government-sponsored Record Commission, in the 1830s the chancery rolls of John's reign began to appear in full and remarkably accurate editions. With their thousands of individual writs and charters, they opened up new 'scientific' perspectives on the birth of Magna Carta.

Even so, the real leap forwards in legal history came from quite another source. Its chief herald was paradoxically the most old-fashioned of 'literary' historians, Thomas Macaulay, author both of a magnificently biased *History of England* and, as presiding law officer in India from 1834 to 1838, of proposals for the reform of Indian criminal law. Macaulay's penal code was written in haste, provoked by the realization that the old East India Company (itself established in 1600 by royal charter) could no longer govern one hundred million subjects using a hotch-potch of laws compounded from regional custom, British parliamentary statute, and Islamic or Hindu religious teachings.

Its success nonetheless proved that laws as ancient and complex as those of India could be reformed and codified. It also suggested that law itself was something closely linked both to history and to social organization (what more modern writers would term 'sociology' or 'social anthropology'). These lessons were taken up by Sir Henry Maine, whose *Ancient Law* (1861) suggested that law and society developed 'from status to contract' and that law itself was not eternal but man-made, subject to precisely those evolutionary twists of fortune that Charles Darwin had already applied to biology and that were now seen to determine the march of political, religious, and social history. Maine himself was a distinguished successor to Macaulay in the administration of the Indian legal system. Ireland, Europe, and the North American continent were already deeply implicated in the history of Magna Carta. India can now be added to this list, assisting the combination of the twin imperatives of law reform and the investigation of the role of past laws into a distinct scholarly subdiscipline, the 'history of law'.

Previous generations had no more dared tamper with Magna Carta than they would have risked altering the text of the Book of Genesis. When it was proposed in the 1660s to move the meeting of the court known as 'The Bench' away from the draughty part of Westminster Hall where it had traditionally met, Chief Justice Bridgman argued, in accordance with an absurdly literal interpretation of Magna Carta, clause 17, that it would be a violation of the charter to move it even 'the distance of an inch'. By the 1830s, efficiency and utility rather than dignity or divine revelation had become the watchwords of the law. Efficiency and utility can indeed be considered the 19th-century equivalents to the old concepts of reason and necessity. Beginning in 1828 with a tentative repeal of clause 36 (clause 26 of the 1225 Magna Carta, on payments for writs), large chunks of Magna Carta began to be chipped away from the statute book. Seventeen of the thirty-seven clauses of the 1225 Magna Carta were repealed in 1863, chiefly relating to 'feudal' incidents. Between 1879 and 1892, a further five clauses disappeared. Clause 18 (clause 7 of the 1225 Magna Carta) was removed in 1925, and clause 26 (clause 18 of the 1225 charter, on debts and testamentary bequests) in 1947. The clauses relating to amercements and fines owed to the king, first heard of as long ago as 1100, in Henry I's coronation charter, enshrined in clauses 20–22 of the 1215 Magna Carta (clause 14 of the 1225 charter), were repealed in 1966. Attempts to repeal the remaining eight clauses then stalled, partly as a result of fears that the entire substructure of English law should not be scraped entirely clean. The constitution should retain not just its efficient but at least some of its more dignified parts. As a result, three and a half clauses (clauses 1, 13, 39, and 40, represented by clauses 1, 9, 29, and part of 37 of the 1225 charter) still remain in English law: barnacles on the great ship of state, of questionable utility save as reminders of how long ago the ship's timbers were first sized and hammered.

Magna Carta thus metamorphized from legislation into historical artefact. Yet its remarkable talent for survival ensures that it continues to make headlines. Together with the Crown Jewels in the Tower of London, and the Houses of Parliament at Westminster, it still constitutes a regular point on the tourist itinerary of London, preserved behind bullet-proof glass in its hermetically sealed capsule in the British Library. Even here, there are surprises. Tourists and the general public often express bewilderment as to why, if the original Magna Carta is preserved in London, they can also view it in Oxford, Salisbury, or Lincoln; in Durham or Hereford, even in Washington or Canberra. This leads us to a topic that still excites confusion. Was there ever an 'original' Magna Carta: the absolutely first version of the settlement, sealed in person by King John? What survive today are the official issues, four of them from the forty or so that must have been written in 1215, and all told twenty-three examples of the issues of 1215, 1216, 1217, 1225, 1297, and 1300. All of these deserve to rank as 'original' Magna Cartas, in the sense that they were all produced in the royal chancery under official supervision.

If there was ever an absolutely 'first' Magna Carta sealed at Runnymede, then it probably vanished long ago. It is possible that a version (preserved today only in a 14th-century copy in the so-called 'Red Book of the Exchequer'), in which Magna Carta is recited by Stephen Langton, the pope's chief envoy and other English and Irish bishops, represents the closest that we will ever come to this 'master' copy.

None of this has deterred the search for an 'original' original. As recently as 1924, for example, it was suggested (in an otherwise sober scholarly article) that slits pierced in the bottom of one of the 1215 Magna Cartas now housed in the British Library were made by King John stabbing the parchment with his dagger: 'the visible evidence of his fury with the barons'. They are in fact nothing of the kind, but traces of the bookbinder's knife, employed when the charter was bound into hard covers back in the 17th century. The desire for direct contact with the past remains a potent modern equivalent to the medieval seeking out of relics and saints' bones as a means of accessing the sacred or charismatic. Of all the documents associated with Magna Carta displayed today, only a few will carry us in a direct, physical sense back to Runnymede and 1215. These were already prized and eagerly collected as long ago as the 17th century, and perhaps long before that. They include the 'Articles of the Barons' (a sealed draft of the eventual treaty, almost certainly produced at Runnymede prior to the final rearrangements and revisions that produced Magna Carta on 15 June). Archbishop Langton seems to have deposited these in his archive at Lambeth Palace. There they remained until the impeachment of Archbishop Laud, from whose papers they were looted. By the 1680s, they were in the possession of Bishop Burnett of Salisbury (who believed them to be Magna Carta itself). They are today in the British Library in London. Also in the British Library, though much less well known, is a short parchment booklet including copies of the coronation charters of Henry I, Stephen, and Henry II, written both in Latin and in Anglo-Norman translations. This too may have been amongst Langton's baggage at Runnymede.

As early as the 1620s, thanks in no small part to the prominence afforded it by the lawyers, Magna Carta was a keenly sought-after trophy. The greatest of the Stuart manuscript collectors, Sir Robert Cotton, forming his library from the detritus of the dissolved medieval monasteries, came into possession of two 'originals' of the 1215 Magna Carta. One of them, ultimate source unknown, he acquired from a London barrister in 1629. It is of particular significance because it seems to represent a half-way house between draft and finished charter, with various clauses and amendments inserted at its foot, apparently introduced only at a late stage in negotiation. The other was part of a great haul of treasures looted by Sir Edward Dering, an east Kent grandee who gained access to the archives of both Canterbury Cathedral and Dover Castle. Dering's 'original' 1215 Magna Carta, sent to Cotton in 1630, probably came from Dover. In 1731, it was badly damaged by fire. Its seal was reduced to a shapeless lump, and although a facsimile was printed with most of the lettering still visible, the text itself has since faded to blank illegibility. It was the facsimile of 1733 that served as the basis for Blackstone's printed text of 1759: the first proper attempt to distinguish between the clauses of the 1215 and 1225 charters. Both of Cotton's Magna Cartas have since entered the national collections, first of the British Museum, subsequently of the British Library.

A third 'original', rumoured in the 18th century to have been preserved at Salisbury Cathedral, was only rediscovered there c. 1812. It presents problems because it is written in a script that seems not to be that of any official chancery scribe. A fourth and final original was brought to light at Lincoln Cathedral, printed in facsimile in the *Statutes of the Realm* in 1810, and henceforth used as the basis for most of the editions of Magna Carta published over the past two centuries. Its particular quality lies in the fact

8. Magna Carta 1215: the Cotton charter, with corrections at the foot

that it is written in an 'official' hand and has remained at Lincoln since the time of its first issue.

Of the subsequent reissues, 'originals' are scattered across the cathedral and college libraries of England. Few institutions bothered to keep a complete series of Magna Cartas, from 1215 through to the final issue of 1300. The only real exception here is Durham Cathedral, which still possesses its originals from 1216, 1225, and 1300. Elsewhere, the general principle seems to have been rather like that applied to modern telephone directories: to acquire the latest version and bin its predecessors. Thus, there are six surviving originals of the 1300 issue (now in the archives of Westminster Abbey, the City of London, Faversham Town Council, Durham Cathedral, and Oriel College and the Bodleian Library at Oxford), more than survive for any previous issue including those of 1215 and 1217, which can boast four examples each. The 1216 reissue, which had legal validity for less than a year, is preserved in a solitary original at Durham. Many of these documents survived as a result of the very obscurity in which they were kept; for example, the 1225 Magna Carta sent into Wiltshire (preserved in the nunnery of Lacock and thence by the post-Reformation owners of Lacock Abbey, the Fox Talbot family), or the 1297 Magna Carta and Forest Charter sent into Surrey (preserved in the archives of an obscure Sussex nunnery and thence scattered by a more recent owner, the Forest Charter to the British Library, the Magna Carta eventually and via a tortuous route to the Australian Parliament in Canberra). There is nothing so conducive to the preservation of historical evidence as benign neglect.

The greatest Magna Carta collections are those housed today in the British Library (which has one 1225 and two 1215 charters besides the original Articles of the Barons), and the Bodleian Library in Oxford (which has three originals of the 1217 issue, one of 1225, and one – perhaps an original, perhaps not – from the issue of 1300). Only two original Magna Cartas are known to exist outside England: that in Canberra, acquired in the 1950s, and the 1297 Magna Carta now displayed in the National Archives at Washington, purchased in the early 1980s by the American billionaire Ross Perot from the Brudenell family of Deene Park in Northamptonshire. This was auctioned in 2007 for the staggering sum of $21.3 million: the highest price ever paid for a single sheet of parchment. During cataloguing for the 2007 sale, at least two Magna Cartas, previously listed as copies, were reidentified as 'originals', and no fewer than four new originals of the Forest Charter came to light. No doubt there are other originals, perhaps of Magna Carta, almost certainly of the Forest Charter, still awaiting discovery, listed as copies or concealed behind catalogue entries describing them merely as 'royal charters'. This was the fate of the Hereford Magna Carta of 1217, catalogued merely as a 'charter of Henry III' and identified as an original Magna Carta as recently as 1989.

Not all has been unruffled calm for Magna Carta in the past century. The 700th anniversary celebrations in 1915 produced what is still the only clause-by-clause commentary, and a flurry of academic articles. Nonetheless, the First World War led to 'Defence of the Realm' regulations that ran entirely contrary to the spirit of Magna Carta clauses 38–40. At the outbreak of the Second World War in 1939, the Lincoln original of the 1215 charter happened to be on display at the New York World's Fair. There, it became the focus of semi-farcical attempts to tip American opinion in favour of the British war effort, with proposals discussed in 1940, backed by Winston Churchill, that it be gifted to the American people. This idea, which would have involved an outright denial of the property rights of the Dean and Chapter of Lincoln, entirely contrary to the spirit of Magna Carta, was eventually shelved, but only after attempts to persuade the British Museum to give up one of its Magna Cartas to be sent to Lincoln as a substitute. Instead, the Lincoln charter spent the War under close guard at Fort Knox. Attempts in 1948 to ensure that the Lacock original of the 1225 Magna

Carta, sent on temporary display to Washington, remain there permanently proved equally fruitless. So did proposals, raised as recently as the American bicentennial in 1976, that the Queen make just such a gift. The fact that the Queen herself owns no original Magna Carta was not the least of the objections to this idea. Ever since the 1770s, there have been demands that 15 June, 'Magna Carta Day', be set aside as a public holiday. A senior British official, asked to comment on one such proposal in 1947, opposed it precisely because it seemed to place liberty above obedience to British rule: 'Colonial peoples might be led into an uncritical enthusiasm for a document which they had not read but which they presumed to contain guarantees of every so-called "right" they might be interested at the moment in claiming.'

From Runnymede to Fort Knox, and from the Roman Empire to the modern industrial state, the story of Magna Carta has taken us far from English medieval law. As its 800th anniversary approaches, Magna Carta continues to command a unique combination of interest and veneration. It still has many mysteries. Remarkable though this may seem, we still do not know who wrote it: its scribes will only be identified when all of the many hundreds of routine documents that King John's chancery issued have been properly collected and assessed. There is still no definitive critical edition that collates all of the various readings of Magna Carta in all of the originals. Equally remarkable, although a clause-by-clause commentary to the 1215 charter was published in the early 20th century (and hence is badly in need of revision), there has never been a clause-by-clause commentary to Magna Carta 1225, even though it is Magna Carta 1225 that entered English law and whose clauses still remain on the statute book. The language of Magna Carta, its references for example to 'liberty', has yet to be properly probed. What precisely was meant by such terms, and do these meanings accord with modern perceptions of 'liberty' or 'law'?

Various of these questions, it is to be hoped, will be answered in the course of the celebrations in 2015. Even then, the mystique will not fade. Frederick Maitland, the greatest of English legal historians, described Magna Carta as a document caught in permanent tension between 'theoretical sanctity and practical insecurity'. In much the same way, modern Runnymede, the place where in George VI's words 'it all started', is a combination of the hallowed and the chaotic: a calm oasis of monuments and water meadow sandwiched uneasily between the M3 motorway and the booming flightpaths of Heathrow Airport. The paradox of modern Runnymede is perhaps a fitting place for us to end our survey of Magna Carta, that most paradoxical yet still most totemic of documentary relics.

Appendix: Magna Carta 1215, an English translation

(Adapted from that in Holt, *Magna Carta* (1992), pp. 448–73)

John, by the grace of God King of England, lord of Ireland, duke of Normandy and Aquitaine, count of Anjou, sends greetings to the archbishops, bishops, abbots, earls, barons, justices, foresters, sheriffs, reeves, ministers and all his bailiffs and faithful subjects. You should know that, at the prompting of God and for the salvation of our soul and the souls of all our ancestors and heirs, for the honour of God and for the exaltation of holy Church and the repair of our realm, through the counsel of our venerable fathers Stephen archbishop of Canterbury, primate of all England and cardinal of the holy Roman church, Henry archbishop of Dublin, William bishop of London, Peter bishop of Winchester, Jocelin bishop of Bath and Glastonbury, Hugh bishop of Lincoln, Walter bishop of Worcester, William bishop of Coventry and Benedict bishop of Rochester, Master Pandulf subdeacon and familiar of the lord Pope, brother Aimery master of the knighthood of the Temple in England, and the noble men William Marshal earl of Pembroke, William earl of Salisbury, William earl Warenne, William earl of Arundel, Alan of Galloway constable of Scotland, Warin fitz Gerald, Peter fitz Herbert, Hubert de Burgh seneschal of Poitou, Hugh de Neville, Matthew fitz Herbert, Thomas Basset, Alan Basset, Philip d'Aubigné, Robert of Ropsley, John Marshal, John fitz Hugh and others of our faithful subjects:

1. We have, in the first place, granted to God and by this our present charter confirmed for ourselves and our heirs in perpetuity that the English Church is to be free and have its rights in whole and its liberties unimpaired, and we wish that this be observed as is evident from the fact that of our own free will, before the dispute that arose between us and our barons, we granted and confirmed by our charter freedom of elections, reputed to be of great importance and most necessary to the English Church, and obtained confirmation of this from the lord Pope Innocent III, which we shall observe and which we wish to be observed by our heirs in perpetuity in good faith.

We have also granted to all the free men of our realm for ourselves and our heirs in perpetuity all the liberties written below, to have and hold to them and their heirs from us and our heirs:

2. If any of our earls or barons or others holding of us in chief by knight service should die, and at his death his heir is of full age and owes relief, he will have his inheritance by the ancient relief, namely the heir or heirs of an earl £100 from a whole earl's barony, the heir or heirs of a baron £100 from a whole barony, and the heir or heirs of a knight at most 100 shillings from a whole knight's fee, and anyone who owes less will give less according to the ancient custom of fees.

3. If, however, the heir of any such person happens to be under age and in custody, when he comes of age he will have his inheritance without relief and without fine.

4. The keeper of the land of such an heir who is under age will not take from the land of the heir anything other than the reasonable issues and reasonable customs and reasonable services, and this without destruction or waste of men or goods. And if we entrust the custody of any such land to a sheriff or to any other who is answerable to us for its issues, and he causes destruction or waste of the custody, we shall take amends of him, and the land will be

committed to two lawful and discreet men of that fee who will answer to us for the issues or to him to whom we shall have assigned them. And if we shall give or sell to anyone the custody of any such land, and he causes destruction or waste, he will lose the custody and it will be transferred to two lawful and discreet men of that fee who will be similarly answerable to us as is aforesaid.

5. The keeper, however, so long as he has custody of the land, will maintain the houses, parks, fishponds, ponds, mills and other things pertaining to that land from the issues of the same land, and he will restore to the heir, when he comes of full age, all his land stocked with ploughs and wainage such as the season of wainage (i.e. the agricultural season) demands, and such as the issues of the land can reasonably support.

6. Heirs will be married without disparagement, save that before a marriage is contracted it be made known to the heir's close kin.

7. After her husband's death, a widow will have her marriage portion and her inheritance at once and without any difficulty, nor will she pay anything for her dower, for her marriage portion, or for her inheritance which she and her husband hold on the day of the said husband's death, and she may stay in her husband's house for forty days after his death, within which period her dower will be assigned to her.

8. No widow will be compelled to marry so long as she wishes to live without a husband, provided that she give security that she will not marry without our consent if she shall hold of us, or without the consent of the lord of whom she holds, if she shall hold of another.

9. Neither we nor our bailiffs shall seize any land or rent in payment of any debt so long as the chattels of the debtor are

sufficient to repay the debt, nor will the sureties of such a debtor be distrained so long as the chief debtor himself is capable of paying the debt, and if the chief debtor defaults in the payment of the debt, having nothing wherewith to pay it, the sureties will be answerable for the debt, and if they wish, they may have the lands and revenues of the debtor until they have received satisfaction for the debt they previously paid on his behalf, unless the chief debtor shows that he has discharged his obligations to the sureties.

10. If anyone who has borrowed from the Jews any amount, great or small, dies before the debt is repaid, it will not carry interest so long as the heir is under age, of whomsoever he holds, and if such debt falls into our hands, we shall take nothing except the chattel specified in the bond.

11. And if a man dies owing a debt to the Jews, his wife is to have her dower and pay nothing for the debt, and if he leaves children under age, their needs will be met in a manner in keeping with the holding of the deceased, and the debt will be paid out of his residue, saving the service due to the lords. Debts owing to others than Jews will be dealt with likewise.

12. No scutage or aid is to be levied in our realm except by the common counsel of our realm, unless it is for the ransom of our body, the knighting of our eldest son, or the first marriage of our eldest daughter, and for these only a reasonable aid is to be levied. Aids from the city of London are to be treated likewise.

13. And the city of London is to have all its ancient liberties and free customs both by land and water. Furthermore, we will and grant that all other cities, boroughs, towns and ports will have all their liberties and free customs.

14. And to obtain the common counsel of the realm for the assessment of an aid, except in the three cases aforesaid, or a scutage, we will have archbishops, bishops, abbots, earls and

greater barons summoned individually by our letters, and we shall also have summoned generally through our sheriffs and bailiffs all those who hold of us in chief, for a fixed date, with at least forty days' notice, and to a fixed place, and in all letters of this summons we shall state the cause for the summons. And when the summons has thus been made, the business will go forward on the assigned day according to the counsel of those present, even if not all those summoned have come.

15. Henceforth we shall not grant anyone that he may take an aid from his free men except to ransom his person, to make his eldest son a knight or to marry his eldest daughter for the first time, and for these purposes only a reasonable aid is to be levied.

16. No man will be compelled to perform more service for a knight's fee or for any other free tenement than is due therefrom.

17. Common pleas will not follow our court but will be held in some fixed place.

18. Recognizances of novel disseisin, mort d'ancestor, and darrein presentment, will not be held elsewhere than in the court of the county in which they occur, and in this manner: we, or if we are out of the realm, our chief justiciar, shall send two justices through each county four times a year, who with four knights of each county chosen by the county will hold the said assizes in the county court on the day and in the place of meeting of the county court.

19. And if the said assizes cannot all be held on the day of the county court, so many knights and freeholders of those present in the county court on that day will remain behind as will suffice to make judgments according to whether the business be great or small.

20. A free man will not be amerced for a trivial offence except in accordance with the degree of the offence, and for a serious offence he will be amerced according to its gravity, saving his livelihood,

and a merchant likewise, saving his merchandise, and in the same way, a villein will be amerced saving his wainage, if they fall into our mercy, and none of the aforesaid amercements will be imposed save by the oath of reputable men of the neighbourhood.

21. Earls and barons will not be amerced except by their peers and only in accordance with the degree of the offence.

22. No clerk will be amerced on his lay tenement except in the manner of the others aforesaid, and without reference to the extent of his ecclesiastical benefice.

23. No vill or man will be forced to build bridges at river banks, except those who ought to do so by tradition and law.

24. No sheriff, constable, coroners or others of our bailiffs will hold pleas of our crown.

25. All shires, hundreds, wapentakes and ridings will be at the ancient farms, without any increment, except our desmesne manors.

26. If anyone holding a lay fief of us dies, and our sheriff or bailiff shows our letters patent of summons for a debt which the deceased owed to us, the sheriff or our bailiff will be allowed to attach and list the chattels of the deceased found in lay fee to the value of that debt, by view of lawful men, so that nothing is removed until the evident debt is paid to us, and the residue will be relinquished to the executors to carry out the will of the deceased. And if he owes us nothing, all the chattels will be accounted as the deceased's, saving their reasonable shares to his wife and children.

27. And if any free man dies intestate, his chattels are to be distributed by his nearest relations and friends, under the supervision of the Church, saving to everyone the debts which the deceased owed him.

28. No constable or any other of our bailiffs will take any man's corn or other chattels unless he pays cash for them at once or can delay payment with the agreement of the seller.

29. No constable is to compel any knight to give money for castle guard, if he is willing to perform that guard in his own person or by another reliable man, if for some good reason he is unable to do it himself, and if we take or send him on military service, he will be excused the guard in proportion to the period of his service in our army.

30. No sheriff or bailiff of ours or anyone else is to take horses or carts of any free man for carting without the free man's agreement.

31. Neither we nor our bailiffs will take other men's timber for castles or other work of ours without the agreement of the owner of the wood.

32. We shall not hold the lands of convicted felons for more than a year and a day, after which the lands will be returned to the lords of the fiefs.

33. Henceforth all fish-weirs will be completely removed from the Thames and the Medway and throughout all England, except on the sea coast.

34. The writ called 'praecipe' will not in future be issued to anyone in respect of any holding whereby a free man might lose his court.

35. Let there be one measure of wine throughout our realm, and one measure of ale and one measure of corn, namely the London quarter, and one width of cloth whether dyed, russet or halberjet, namely two ells within the selvedges. Let it be the same with weights as with measures.

36. Henceforth, nothing will be given or taken for the writ of inquisition of life or limb, but it will be given freely and not refused.

37. If anyone holds of us by fee-farm, by socage or by burgage, and holds land of someone else by knight service, we shall not, by virtue of that fee-farm, socage or burgage, have custody of his heir or of land of his that belongs to the fief of another, nor shall we have custody of that fee-farm or socage or burgage unless such fee-farm owes knight service. We shall not have custody of the heir or land of anyone who holds of another by knight service by virtue of any petty serjeanty which he holds of us by the service of rendering to us knives or arrows or the like.

38. Henceforth, no bailiff will put anyone on trial by his own unsupported allegation, without bringing credible witnesses to the charge.

39. No free man will be taken or imprisoned or disseised or outlawed or exiled or in any way ruined, nor shall we go or send against him, save by the lawful judgement of his peers and by the law of the land.

40. To no one shall we sell, to no one shall we deny or delay right or justice.

41. All merchants are to be safe and secure in leaving and entering England, and in staying and travelling in England both by land and by water, to buy and sell free from all bad tolls, by the ancient and rightful customs, except in time of war and if such merchants come from a land at war against us. And if such are found in our land at the outbreak of war, they will be detained without damage to their persons or goods until we or our chief justiciar know how the merchants of our land are treated in the country at war against us, and if ours are safe there, the others will be safe in our land.

42. Henceforth anyone, saving his allegiance due to us, may leave our realm and return safe and secure by land and water, save for a short period in time of war on account of the general interest of the realm and excepting those imprisoned and outlawed according to the law of the realm, and natives of a land at war against us, and merchants who will be treated as aforesaid.

43. If anyone dies who holds of some escheat such as the honours of Wallingford, Nottingham, Boulogne or Lancaster or of other escheats which are in our hands and are baronies, his heir will not give any relief or do any service to us other than what he would have done to the baron if that barony had been in a baron's hands, and we shall hold it in the same manner as the baron held it.

44. Henceforth men who live outside the forest will not come before our justices of the forest upon a general summons, unless they are impleaded or are sureties for any person or persons who are attached for forest offences.

45. We shall not make justices, constables, sheriffs or bailiffs who do not know the law of the realm and wish to observe it well.

46. All barons who have founded abbeys of which they have charters of the kings of England or ancient tenure will have custody thereof during vacancies as they ought to have.

47. All forests which have been afforested in our time will be disafforested at once, and river banks which we have enclosed in our time will be treated similarly.

48. All evil customs of forests and warrens, foresters and warreners, sheriffs and their servants, river banks and their wardens are to be investigated at once in every county by twelve sworn knights of the same county who should be chosen by worthy men of the county, and within forty days of the inquiry such bad customs are to be abolished by them beyond recall,

provided that we or our justiciar, if we are not in England, first know of it.

49. We shall restore at once all hostages and charters delivered to us by Englishmen as securities for peace or faithful service.

50. We shall dismiss completely from their offices the relations of Girard d'Athée that henceforth they will have no office in England, (namely) Engelard de Cigogné, Peter and Guy and Andrew de Chanceaux, Guy de Cigogné, Geoffrey de Martigny with his brothers, Philip Mark with his brothers and his nephew Geoffrey and all their followers.

51. And immediately after restoring peace, we shall remove from the realm all alien knights, crossbowmen, sergeants and mercenaries who have come with horses and arms to the injury of the realm.

52. If anyone has been disseised or deprived by us without lawful judgement of his peers of lands, castles, liberties or his right, we shall restore them to him at once, and if any disagreement arises on this, then let it be settled by the judgement of the twenty-five barons referred to below in the clause securing the peace. But for all those things of which anyone was disseised or deprived without lawful judgement of his peers by King Henry (II) our father or by King Richard (I) our brother, which we hold in our hand or which are held by others under our warranty, we shall have respite for the usual crusader's term, excepting those cases in which a plea was begun or inquest made on our order before we took the cross. When we return, however, from our pilgrimage, or if perhaps we do not undertake it, we shall at once do full justice in these matters.

53. We shall have the same respite, and in the same manner, in doing justice on disafforesting or retaining those forests which Henry (II) our father or Richard (I) our brother afforested,

and concerning custody of lands which are of the fee of another, the which custodies we have hitherto by virtue of a fee held of us by knight's service, and concerning abbeys founded on fees other than our own, in which the lord of the fee claims to have a right. And as soon as we return, or if we do not undertake our pilgrimage, we shall at once do full justice to complainants in these matters.

54. No one will be taken or imprisoned upon the appeal of a woman for the death of anyone except her husband.

55. All fines which were made with us unjustly and contrary to the law of the land, and all amercements made unjustly and contrary to the law of the land, will be completely remitted or else they will be settled by the judgement of the twenty-five barons mentioned below in the clause securing the peace, or by the judgement of the majority of the same, acting with the aforesaid Stephen archbishop of Canterbury if he can be present, and others whom he wishes to summon with him for this purpose. And if he cannot be present, the business will nevertheless proceed without him, provided that if any one or more of the aforesaid twenty-five barons are implicated in such a suit, they will stand down in this particular judgement and will be replaced by others chosen and sworn in by the rest of the same twenty-five for this case only.

56. If we have disseised or deprived Welshmen of lands, liberties or other things without lawful judgement of their peers in England or in Wales, they are to be returned to them at once, and if a dispute arises over this, it will be settled in the March by judgement of their peers for tenements in England according to the law of England, and for tenements in Wales according to the law of Wales, and for tenements in the March according to the law of the March. The Welsh are to do the same for us and ours.

57. For all those things, however, of which any Welshman has been disseised or deprived without lawful judgement of his peers by King

Henry (II) our father or King Richard (I) our brother, which we have in our hands or which others hold under our warranty, we shall have respite for the usual crusader's term, excepting those cases in which a plea was begun or inquest made on our order before we took the cross. However, when we return, or if perhaps we do not go on pilgrimage, we shall at once give them full justice in accordance with the laws of the Welsh and the aforesaid regions.

58. We shall restore at once the son of Llewylyn and all the hostages from Wales and the charters delivered to us as security for peace.

59. We shall treat with Alexander King of the Scots concerning the return of his sisters and hostages and his liberties and right in the same manner in which we act towards our other barons of England, unless it ought to be otherwise because of the charters which we have from William his father, formerly King of the Scots, and this will be determined by the judgement of his peers in our court.

60. All these aforesaid customs and liberties which we have granted to be held in our realm as far as pertains to us towards our men will be observed by all men of our realm, both clerks and laymen, as far as pertains to them towards their own men.

61. Since, moreover, we have granted all the aforesaid things for God, for the repair of our realm and the better settling of the dispute which has arisen between us and our barons, wishing these things to be enjoyed fully and undisturbed in perpetuity, we give and grant them the following security, namely that the barons will choose any twenty-five barons of the realm they wish, who with all their might ought to observe, maintain and cause to be observed the peace and liberties that we have granted and confirmed to them by this our present charter, so that if we or our justiciar or our bailiffs or any other of our ministers offend against anyone in any way, or transgress any of the articles of peace or security, and the offence is

shown to four of the aforesaid twenty-five barons, those four will
come to us or our justiciar, if we are out of the realm, and will bring it
to our notice and ask that we have it redressed without delay. And if
we, or our justiciar, should we be out of the realm, do not redress the
offence within forty days from the time when it was brought to the
notice of us or our justiciar, should we be out of the realm, then the
aforesaid four barons will refer the case to the rest of the twenty-five
barons, and those twenty-five barons with the commune of all the
land will distrain and distress us in every way they can, namely by
seizing castles, lands and possessions, and in such other ways as they
can, saving our person and those of our queen and of our children,
until, in their judgement, amends have been made, and when it has
been redressed, they are to obey us as they did before. And anyone in
the land who wishes may take an oath to obey the orders of the said
twenty-five barons in the execution of all the aforesaid matters, and
to join with them in distressing us to the best of his ability, and we
publicly and freely permit anyone who wishes to take the oath, and
we shall never forbid anyone to take it. Moreover, we shall compel
and order all those in the land who of themselves and of their own
free will are unwilling to take an oath to the twenty-five barons to
distrain and distress us with them, to take the oath as aforesaid. And
if any of the twenty-five barons dies or leaves the land or is otherwise
prevented from discharging these aforesaid duties, the rest of the
aforesaid twenty-five barons will on their own decision choose
another in his place who will take the oath in the same way as the
others. In all matters the execution of which is committed to those
twenty-five barons, if it should happen that the twenty-five are
present and disagree amongst themselves on anything, or if any of
them who has been summoned will not come or cannot come,
whatever the majority of those present may provide or order is to be
taken as fixed and settled as if the whole twenty-five had agreed to it,
and the aforesaid twenty-five are to swear that they will faithfully
observe all the aforesaid and will do all they can to secure its
observance. And we will procure nothing from anyone, either
personally or through another, by which any of these concessions
and liberties will be revoked or diminished, and if any such thing is

procured it will be null and void, and we shall never use it either ourselves or through another.

62. And we have fully remitted and pardoned to all any ill will, grudge or rancour that have arisen between us and our subjects, clerk or lay, from the time of the dispute. Moreover, we have fully remitted and fully pardoned to all, clerk and lay, as far as pertains to us, all offences occasioned by the said dispute from Easter in the sixteenth year of our reign to the conclusion of peace. And moreover we have caused testimonial letters patent of the lord Stephen, archbishop of Canterbury, and the lord Henry, archbishop of Dublin, the aforesaid bishops and Master Pandulf to be made for them on this security and the aforesaid concessions.

63. Wherefore we wish and firmly command that the English Church will be free, and the men in our realm will have and hold all the aforesaid liberties, rights and concessions well and peacefully, freely and quietly, fully and completely for themselves and their heirs of us and our heirs in all things and places for ever, as is aforesaid. Moreover, an oath has been sworn, both on our part and on the part of the barons, that all these things aforesaid will be observed in good faith and without evil intent. Witness the abovementioned and many others. Given by our hand in the meadow that is called Runnymede between Windsor and Staines, on the fifteenth day of June in the seventeenth year of our reign.

Further reading

The classic study remains that by J. C. Holt, *Magna Carta*, first
published in 1964, now in its second edition (1992). Holt's *The
Northerners* (1961, second edition 1992) is indispensable for the
history of John's reign, and offers a very good read.

Amongst the small library of books dedicated to the subject, I have
made particular use of Faith Thompson, *Magna Carta: Its Role in
the Making of the English Constitution* (1948), and Anne Pallister's
sparkling *Magna Carta: The Heritage of Liberty* (1971).

For background histories of Angevin England, David Carpenter's *The
Struggle for Mastery: Britain, 1066-1284* (2003), and Nicholas
Vincent, *A Brief History of Britain: The Making of the Nation
1066-1485* (2011) offer a framework. The classic study remains
(the crabbed, bizarre, but still compelling) J. E. A. Jolliffe, *Angevin
Kingship* (1955), written by an Oxford academic in almost total
isolation from other modern approaches, yet informed by a deep
understanding of the charisma of tyrants acquired both at Keble
College Oxford and during Jolliffe's war service in Brazil.

The best of the modern biographies of King John is that by W. L.
Warren, *King John* (1961), with a significant collection of essays
edited by Stephen Church, *King John: New Interpretations* (1999).

The history of medieval law has tended to develop as an arcane
science, closed to enquiries from *hoi polloi*. There are nonetheless
introductions that will lead readers as far as the temple gates, by
John Hudson in his two books, *Land, Law and Lordship in
Anglo-Norman England* (1994) and *The Formation of the English
Common Law* (1996), and by Bruce O'Brien, *God's Peace and
King's Peace: The Laws of Edward the Confessor* (1999). For a

particularly revealing history of the meaning of 'liberty' to those living both before and after the Norman Conquest, see Julia Crick, '"Pristina Libertas": Liberty and the Anglo-Saxons Revisited', *Transactions of the Royal Historical Society*, 6th ser. 14 (2004): 47–71. There is much that is essential expounded in essays by John Maddicott, 'Magna Carta and the Local Community 1215-1259', *Past and Present*, 102 (1984): 25–65; David Carpenter, in various of the essays in his *The Reign of Henry III* (1996); and by Paul Brand in his collection *The Making of the Common Law* (1992). The adventurous are recommended to return to the grandfather of modern legal history, Frederick William Maitland, whose *History of English Law* (2 vols, 1895; several modern reprints) is not only as learned but a great deal better written than much that has followed it.

The material above relating to the reissues and documentary history of Magna Carta is derived from the survey I carried out in 2007 for the sale of Magna Carta in New York, published, with lavish photographic reproductions, as *The Magna Carta* (Sotheby's Sale Catalogue, New York, 18 December 2007). One bizarre subhistory here is told in greater detail in my booklet *Australia's Magna Carta*, published by the Australian Senate (2010).

Index

M